# THE OPEN-BOOK
# MANAGEMENT
# FIELD BOOK

# THE OPEN-BOOK MANAGEMENT FIELD BOOK

John P. Schuster
Jill Carpenter
M. Patricia Kane

John Wiley & Sons, Inc.

New York • Chichester • Weinheim • Brisbane • Singapore • Toronto

This text is printed on acid-free paper.

Copyright © 1998 by John P. Schuster, Jill Carpenter, and M. Patricia Kane.
Published by John Wiley & Sons, Inc.

This publication is designed to provide accurate and authoritative
information in regard to the subject matter covered. It is sold with
the understanding that the publisher is not engaged in rendering legal,
accounting, or other professional services. If legal advice or other expert
assistance is required, the services of a competent professional person
should be sought.

**Library of Congress Cataloging-in-Publication Data:**

Schuster, John P.
   The open-book management field book  /  John P. Schuster, Jill
Carpenter, M. Patricia Kane.
      p.    cm.
   Includes index.
   ISBN 0-471-18036-X (pbk. : alk. paper)
   1. Management—Employee participation.   2. Open-book management.
I. Carpenter, Jill, 1943–    .  II. Kane, M. Patricia.   III. Title.
   HD5650.S3964 1997
  658.3'152—dc21                                     97-23164

Printed in the United States of America

10  9  8  7  6  5  4  3  2  1

To the workers of the twenty-first century,
across the world, in rice fields, in board rooms,
behind computers, in factories and restaurants.
May they produce more, with more dignified toil, and
be rewarded financially and in spirit,
as full-fledged participants in an open-book planet.
May each experience the pride and satisfaction that goes with
making a contribution to a flourishing enterprise.

To open-book entrepreneurs and leaders
who dare to see and think differently,
to challenge themselves and their colleagues
to chart new potential for their businesses.

# *Acknowledgments*

As we developed the concept for a field book on open-book management, and as it grew through the prompting of our editor at John Wiley & Sons, Jeanne Glasser, we became very aware of a central fact: This book is, in large measure, a creation of the people practicing open-book management. In the summer of 1996, we put out a call to our friends, clients, open-book veterans, and newcomers to give us the specifics of their stories.

And they did. For several months, our fax machines and E-mail in-box filled with the stories—the forms and thoughts that comprise most of the examples in this book. To all these contributors, we owe a debt of gratitude:

- Our special thanks to Rob Zicaro for his well-constructed front-line insights on how open-book management at Web Converting works and how it has changed his life.
- Very special thanks to Steve Sheppard and the entire team at Foldcraft, an awesome example of an enterprise that acts as a learning community, and for living Player-Coach Leadership in its highest forms.
- Our new partner Mary Hansen, for her gifts with numbers and great work helping clients become more business literate and for her contributions to Chapters 6 and 7.
- Patrick Maynard, a leader at United Cerebral Palsy in Seattle and Cathy Kramer and Amy Katz

at The Association for Quality and Participation, for providing business literacy leadership in not-for-profit environments, and for the opportunity to present at the annual conventions and the School for Managing.

- Tim O'Donnell, publisher of *Olathe* (Kansas) *Daily News* for sharing his leadership journey. Sue Rye at Tell City Indiana bank for the great compilation of their Profit and Cash® results; MANCO's Kevin Kreuger, Jack Kahl, and Cheryl Dimattia for the MANCO stories.
- Mark Stewart and the employees of Schrock Cabinet Company for their getting-started story, including their bonus plan ideas; Chris Kuehl for the economic expertise and imagination to see the big picture of where this is all headed.
- Judy Friefield, controller at the HSM Group for her persistent and careful stewardship of her company's numbers.
- The many leaders at Syncrude Canada, Ltd., in Alberta—Phil Lachambre, Jim Carter, Derrick Kershaw, Don de Guerre—for demonstrating clearly the powerful business results when open-book management is used to connect investor and employee interests; for their thoughtful interpretations of how creating a line of sight and business literacy in their oil sands operation supports their long-term strategy.
- All our coworkers—Linda Jones, Mechille Parker, Cyndi Rue, David Stookey, and Donna Ziegenhorn, for entrepreneuring and keeping the faith.
- Meek and Associates, a consulting firm specializing in incentive and performance-based pay, Chapter 7 includes some of their thinking.
- Gary Rosentreter at Advo, Inc., for his belief in the power of business education.

- Our new strategic partners, American Express Tax and Business Services, Inc. formerly known as Checkers, Simon & Rosner, for their vision and knowledge of the business promise to lead those looking for open-book assistance. Thanks to Jerome A. Harris (Chapter 6), Les Hoffman, Jeff Balkan, John Lincoln, John Liberman, John Karnatz, and his colleagues in the Business Technology Group for pioneering and digging in.
- J. Beyster and his colleagues at the Foundation for Enterprise Development for their support and ideas.
- Bob Rogers and the entrepreneurial team at the Kauffman Foundation for their unique contributions to business and learning, and teaming with us on innovative projects.
- Bob Argabright, a great open-book leader, for sharing his expertise with our clients and his thoughts for our book (Chapter 7).
- Ann Bradley, Kathy Gore, and their colleagues at Central and Southwest Services, Inc. who co-created a utility version of Profit and Cash® and for their courage in seeking new methods to create business thinkers within a regulated environment.
- Russ Pflasterer and the team at the Electric Power Research Institute for the opportunity to create power generation versions of our financial literacy tools and John Browning at UtiliCorp United for putting Russ up to the idea.

We would also like to salute the following people:

- Nora Andersen and her colleagues at Honeywell and Phil Casey and his management team at Ameristeel. Marcus Brown at Williams Pipeline, Earl Estes at Virginia Power, Dick Edwards, Tom

Lien, Ken Kuene, John Trover and the team at Amax Coal. Their journeys will create the next chapter of open-book accomplishments.

- Mark Tezak, Dwayne Brinkman, and Steve Gibbons at Principal Financial for the curiosity and commitment to bring business literacy to their internal customers. The "Working for Profitability" Team at BCHydro's Power Supply Business Unit including Cherly Bucar, Janice Heslop, Phil Webber, Bob Abernathy, Linda Koopman, and Jan MacLain.

# Contents

# Introduction

In 1993, during what was perhaps the heyday of the Total Quality movement, we asked a question of the attendees at a metal parts manufacturer's conference in Tucson: "How many of you have a quality process in place at your company?" Impressively, over 95 percent of the hands went up. Then we asked: "How many of you are *deeply* into quality?" The number of raised hands dwindled to about 5 percent.

Total Quality had been a major movement in American management and yet it seemed to have made barely a dent in the corporate psyche. What had happened? In the words of one of our consultant colleagues: "Many organizations caught a mild form of quality and are now immune to the real thing." Something great that might have been was lost, replaced by a shadow of itself.

Unfortunately many new management tools, methods, and philosophies—re-engineering, for example—meet the same fate. They are introduced to great acclaim, only to fall rapidly into disuse, misuse, or underuse. We have all seen organizations take a sound set of principles, and through misapplication, do more harm than good. Many a promising process has fallen on the dung heap of discredited programs, leaving managers and employees ticked-off, disillusioned, and a little more cynical.

## WHY THIS FIELD BOOK?

Our fervent hope and goal is to prevent open-book management (OBM) from meeting the same fate. To help the business community bridge that sometimes cavernous gap between promising theory and effective practice, we are extremely excited to be offering this field book. Many people—clients, consultants, and academics—felt that our first book, *The Power of Open-Book Management: Releasing the True Potential of People's Minds, Hearts, and Hands* (John Wiley, 1996), filled a real need, capturing both the fundamentals and complexity of the subject. But during the 18 months since we completed the book, we've noticed definite, disturbing parallels between the current popularity of open-book management and many organizations' former fascination with total quality or re-engineering.

In our consulting travels, describing the systems of open-book management and helping companies institute practices, a couple of things became crystal clear. First, the change that open-book management requires is deep and, for many, enormously challenging. Open-book management practices fly in the face of old and firmly rooted divisions between workers and managers. And second, the rewards that OBM practices can produce are, at times, nothing short of miraculous. Every day, ordinary people are turning their companies into fun, financially vibrant businesses.

As we worked with and continued to hear from open-book management practitioners, we gained respect for the fact that open-book management is a work in progress, and much of that progress is taking place in the field, at companies like yours. That was the inspiration for this book: to offer a compendium of applied theory and real-life experience that shows the state of the OBM art, how it's being practiced and adapted, what results it is achieving and, most of all, how you can apply it successfully in your own company.

We want to encourage managers and company owners not to stop with the milder forms of open-book philosophy—which can be potent in their own right—but instead push business literacy to its full potential, realizing the deepest gains possible from creating a company of business thinkers.

## How to Read This Book

This book can stand on its own as a primer for newcomers to or veterans of open-book management. Or it can be read as a companion to our first book on the subject, *The Power of Open-Book Management.* As a field book, it provides less theory and more examples, less overview and more detail than its predecessor.

The book is divided into two sections. Section One contains a summary of the theory and principles of open-book management as we have defined them. It delineates the four key dimensions of our open-book model, addresses the importance and payoffs of the open-book concept in the context of the emerging worldwide economy, and tells you how to gauge and enhance your company's preparedness to go open-book. This acts as a basis for our extensive discussions in Section Two, where each chapter is devoted to the practical application of one of our key OBM dimensions (Critical Numbers Know-How, The Intensive Huddle System, No-Kidding Ownership, and Player-Coach Leadership). Section Two is where you get to see what is really working in the field and how you can make it work similarly at your company.

Although it is generally most useful to read this book from Chapter 1 through Chapter 8, each chapter has an internal logic and can be approached individually. Additionally, there are a number of recurring themes and devices that will allow you to use this book in a number of ways and give it the feel of a living document:

**The Icons.** In Section Two, three icons are used to call your attention to certain types of information:

**FIELD NOTES**

**Field Notes.** This icon appears when we are using a real-life example to illustrate how an open-book principle is being put into practice.

**VOICES**

**Voices.** This icon indicates a verbatim quotation from an open-book practitioner providing an insight or lesson learned from implementing OBM.

**HANDS-ON LESSONS**

**Hands-On Lessons.** This icon appears when we describe exercises readers can use with their teams to develop open-book systems and measure their progress.

☑ **The Survey.** To shed some statistical light on the theories and anecdotal evidence we present to make the open-book case, we surveyed more than 80 companies of all sizes and got responses from 101 different managers. The biggest companies are Fortune 1000 entries that we know well because they are clients, and the great majority of the smaller companies (with fewer than 500 employees) are members of San Diego-based The Executive Committee (TEC) which has 3,500 CEO-members in the United States. We wanted to find out what they were doing and *how* they were doing with open-book management.

The results appear throughout the book to bolster the points being made in each chapter. (The complete survey results can be found in Appendix II.)

- **The People.** If there are protagonists in this book, they are Rob Zicaro and Steve Sheppard. They are the book's two most prominent and prolific contributors. Rob is a machine operator at Web Converting in Framingham, Massachusetts. Steve is CEO of Foldcraft, makers of furniture for large institutions and restaurants, located in Kenyon, Minnesota. We refer to both men as "philosophers" and "conscious competents," meaning that they are deep and reflective thinkers, able to make sense of and articulate the processes and benefits of open-book management at their companies, both of which have been open-book for many years. Their voices are the wise and witty Greek chorus of our book.

But there are many other voices in this book: four of the 3,500 employees who successfully embraced the business literacy process at Syncrude Canada, Ltd., the oil company that mines the oil sands in northern Alberta, Canada; and employees of small consulting firms, a community newspaper, a large utility, a telecommunications firm, and a host of other companies that had valuable experiences to share.

These companies and their open-book leaders make the ideas and theory of business literacy and open-book management snap, crackle, and pop into three-dimensional business excitement and learning. From the nitty-gritty measures of machine operators to the leadership musings of executives, open-book management kaleidoscopes itself into view through these very committed and very human individuals trying to make a living and a livelihood worthwhile for themselves and their customers and coworkers.

We hope you enjoy this book and find it useful. We invite you to interact with us about the book or your learning experiences with open-book management. Phone us, send us an E-mail, or check out our website, www.capital-connections.com. Good luck!

*John, Jill, Patricia, and the Capital Connections team*

Capital Connections
801 W 47th St. #411
Kansas City, Missouri 64112
816-561-6622
800-883-4263
*www.capcon@swbell.net*

*Section One*

# PRINCIPLES
# AND
# PREPARATION

# 1

## The Open-Book Future

### Why OBM Is Important and How It Pays Off

*People come to work as whole human beings, not machines without brains or emotions. Open-book management is not used as a punitive tool to command and control people; it's real power enables people to participate in and control improvements to their work through self-directed decision making and autonomy. The power to have a voice and a say in how their company performs financially, connects people to the business in a deeper sense, cultivating a competitive advantage as workers take control of their economic destiny.*

Rob Zicaro,
Machine Operator
Web Converting

In most companies today, the answer to the question "Who runs the business?" is: "the president," or "the senior management team." The answer in open-book management companies is: "We all do."

Open-book management is a different way of thinking about business and all its component parts. Its simple requirement is that employees at all levels take full responsibility for "running" their part of the process well, not as a cog in a machine, but thinking and acting intelligently, fully informed, and fully aligned with the goals of the company.

Simply put, open-book management is an interlocking system of daily result-focused practices, incentive structures, information-sharing and decision-making mechanisms and teamwork principles. The result is a company of business-smart people whose efforts are constantly aligned in pursuit of a single goal: the maximum generation and distribution of wealth.

When asked to help our clients with their open-book management efforts, we discover that most have read the business press about OBM, but have only a partial understanding.

The vast majority of companies practicing open-book management have been at it for fewer than three years (see Figure 1–1). In our analysis, we've found that they are implementing in a piecemeal fashion—usually a bonus system and some numbers sharing—but not the total approach. Many have not evolved a complete system including companywide financial training and sophisticated teamwork and communication.

They have often used training and education programs as an important part of start-up, to get everyone

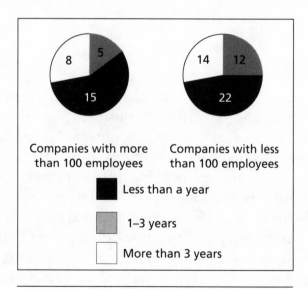

Companies with more      Companies with less
than 100 employees        than 100 employees

■ Less than a year

▨ 1–3 years

□ More than 3 years

**Figure 1–1.** Number of years practicing OBM.

oriented to an open-book approach and to the company's business goals. But after the initial phase of adoption, continuous real-time learning mechanisms must be put in place to respond to the company's changing business needs. In our Business Literacy Capital Connections, Inc. model (Figure 1–2), these mechanisms are the four basic dimensions of OBM. They are management practices, not training programs.

1. *Critical Numbers Know-How.* Educating all employees about the critical financial numbers and ratios that measure and drive performance in their company; they must know, individually and as a team, how to influence those numbers positively; they must connect their day-to-day thinking and actions to how their company makes money.

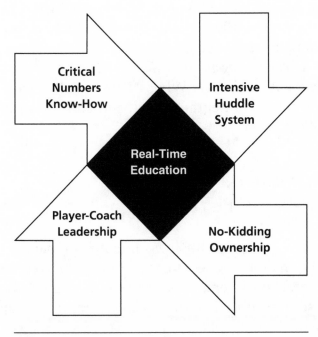

**Figure 1–2.** Business literacy model.

2. *The Intensive Huddle System.* Imparting current, abundant, and accurate information and training to all employees; there must be institutionalized ways for information to be routinely and frequently communicated in all directions.

3. *No-Kidding Ownership.* Giving each employee a *real* financial stake in the company's success, in the form of variable pay, profit sharing, or equity that is tied to the company's common and unifying goals such as profitability or economic value added.

4. *Player/Coach Leadership.* Empowering all employees to show leadership, but especially those in key roles who must take primary responsibility for focusing day-to-day actions and decisions on companywide goals.

These are the four pillars on which an open-book company is built. In Section Two of this book, we examine how these dimensions play out in the field, how they are applied on a day-to-day practical level at real companies like yours.

*Open-book management is the simultaneous application of these four disciplines.* When OBM is fully realized, each of them is integrated with and enhances the effect of the others.

## A GLIMPSE INTO THE OPEN-BOOK FUTURE

The drive to create business-literate companies has just begun and will be here for a long time to come, in part because the open-book approach meshes nicely with several other healthy business trends: intrapreneurism, incentive-based pay structures pegged to companywide results, flexible, organic work environments, and team-based communication and execution. The open-book approach is so right on so many levels for the times in which we live, that we expect it will not only be adopted rapidly over the coming decades, but it will be *internalized.* There will be less and less to discuss or debate. It will simply become the way business is run.

Here are just some of the dramatic and revolutionary developments we see complementing or arising from the increasing application of open-book management systems:

- *The Spread of Global Capitalism.* As the different and emerging forms of capitalism around the world encounter this Americanized version of open-book capitalism, cultures will make their own adaptations of concepts and processes. "Open-book management is a tool that is particularly relevant to the increasing pace of global economic change and the emergence of new economies transitioning from various forms of central planning and control," asserts economist Chris Kuehl. "While companies in the United States have tended to focus exclusively on their stockholders and owners and have defined their mission according to what best meets the needs of this group . . . many nations demand that the business community become integrated in the goals of the entire system they are a part of. The use of open-book management is ideally suited for systems in which accurate information needs to be shared with a larger community."

- *The Continued Rise of Smaller Companies.* As it evolves domestically and overseas, OBM will continue to be driven by smaller, more flexible companies (and the entrepreneurial divisions and units of larger companies) that can "get their arms around all of their systems" and have a tight feedback loop among all departments and including customers.

- *The Increasing Availability of Information.* The revolution in information systems will hasten—and be hastened by—the open-book concept of real-time education by making instant results available. Intranet systems will allow access to sales, operating, profit, customer, and quality numbers as events happen. The super integration of systems will continue to create boundaryless information transfer that will be a commonplace occurrence. But boundaryless and boundless information is not an advantage if it drowns employees in waves of endless noise. CEOs as chief learning officers have a lot of teaching and coaching to do, recognizing that having financial data at everyone's fingertips is not a competitive advantage until employees can act on the data. That takes education.

- *Greater Investment in Human Capital.* Since the critical ingredient to open-book management is business and financial literacy for all employees, the system's growing success will spearhead a trend toward substantial investments in learning and training among small and large companies alike.

- *The Competitive Advantage of Empowerment.* Competitive advantage will be enjoyed by the open-book companies who better focus employee effort and innovative responses to the marketplace. Companies that understand the brainpower left on the table by not using open-book practices are the ones that will win out. Open-book environments create an alignment between customers and employees, between employees and shareholders, so new ideas and approaches are the norm, not the exception. The inherent win-win in business literate companies and the real-time connection between marketplace shifts and the teams responding to the shifts equips open-book companies with an arsenal others can't match.

- *The Emphasis on Efficient Enterprise.* The industries farthest behind will make the most bold moves with open-book management. We sense the sleeping giants—the industries that have done little with open-book theory compared to manufacturing and the highly competitive parts of the service sector—have a great need for business literacy and will move ahead of other sectors in adopting the practices. Two that we think are getting ready to do so are the health care and utilities industries. The pressure to deregulate the utility industry and to get on sound financial footing to play in a competitive marketplace makes the efficiency and effectiveness of the open-book approach particularly relevant. Furthermore, we fully expect government and not-for-profit enterprises to get on the bandwagon.

- *Leveraging the Mobile Workforce.* Open-book companies will have a recruiting advantage as they create an environment for career and professional growth that traditional bureaucracies can't match. As long-term job stability increasingly becomes a thing of the past, open-book companies will be fostering business skills, employability, lateral career moves, and the personal responsibility that the new workforce will list as a must.

- *The Overriding Importance of Leadership.* We will revisit this theme again and again in this book. In the twenty-first century, the success of any enterprise, its vibrancy, relevancy, and competitive advantage will be determined, more than any other factor, by the quality of its leadership. Open-book management is a system of systems that, by its very nature, conspires to create a company of leaders. That in itself guarantees that OBM is no fad. On the contrary, it is quickly becoming the way business must be done.

## How Can OBM Help Your Company Meet the Challenges?

In the context of the seismic socioeconomic shifts we've been discussing, you have to be asking yourself: Why would I adopt OBM—what business results am I after? There are a number of persuasive reasons to adopt an open-book management approach in the current business environment. Here are the most common and most convincing, each bolstered by voices from the field which testify to the efficacy of OBM in achieving the desired outcome:

- *OBM Can Help Achieve Growth.* When an enterprise is planning to diversify its product offerings, to grow its market share or customer base, open-book management systems help employees understand the challenges associated with business growth and the contribution they need to make to its successful outcome. In times of expansion and flux, there is enormous value and stability in reinforcing a focus on the specific activities and decisions that relate directly to the critical growth numbers.

Patrick Kelly, CEO of Physician Sales and Service in Tampa, Florida, uses his open-book education and information system as the cement for the foundation of the company's fast-growth culture:

"As we grow with acquisitions, the way we ensure a consistency across all the sites is to install our process of opening the books. Some managers and employees get it right away and others take a little longer. But without a doubt, we couldn't grow this fast and keep order, or motivate everyone in the same direction, if we didn't take an open-information approach so we can see what we are all doing."

VOICES

- *OBM Can Improve Financial Performance.* If earnings are stagnant, expenses are increasing too fast, revenue is slow, return on assets or equity isn't satisfactory, open-book management is a great fit. Its emphasis on awareness of essential numbers and ratios will help you identify the key lever to success and focus each individual on what he or she needs to achieve to hit the overall target.

Judy Friefield, controller at HSM, a small health care-related service company in Scottsdale, Arizona, expresses it this way:

"HSM's goals in implementing open-book management were to give all of our employees the feeling that what they do impacts the success of the company and to give them a sense of ownership. We wanted to promote employee loyalty, provide a means of increasing revenues and profits, provide a means of compensating everyone fairly, and to address productivity problems with a team approach rather than a top-down approach. The results that we are targeting are gross revenues and net profit as a percentage of revenue. We also have a minimum cash balance goal which takes into account the liquidity issue and a minimum profit level to cover the situation where we could have very low revenues but still be very profitable. Our bonuses are heavily weighted toward the profitability goal, rather than the gross revenue goal."

VOICES

Such targets correlate with the desired outcomes only when employees have knowledge, the authority to act on that knowledge, and a *stake in the outcome* of their actions. When a company is privately owned and the primary motive of the owner(s) is to increase his or her own wealth, open-book management is not likely to work. Likewise, in a publicly traded company, if the motive is only to improve the stock price and/or dividend pay out, with mainly the CEO, a few senior officers, and shareholders reaping the reward then open-book management will not last. The employees won't care to work harder and smarter so someone else can get richer.

### ☑ SURVEY

Capital Connections' Survey on Open-Book Management (see Appendix) reveals in some detail what open-book management companies identify as the benefits they receive. By far, the most frequently named advantages were teamwork, pride, and alignment of results to compensation programs. For those companies that had been practicing open-book management for more than three years, financial results improved regularly.

The survey also shows that the companies that get off to the best start are those whose leaders can articulate a *compelling, measurable* business reason to employ open-book management and buy into a philosophy of human potential which is the foundation of open-book thinking.

- *OBM Can Increase Investor Returns.* If your company needs to attract new investors or retain the confidence of current investors, an open-book approach can link employee interests to investor interests through the establishment of substantive gain sharing practices. For an excellent illustration of how this can happen, listen to Phil Lachambre, CFO and vice president of Business and Corporate Affairs of Syncrude, Canada, Ltd. in Ft. McMurray, Alberta:

"We have a lot of large numbers at Syncrude. When an employee hears that our operation generated $330 million in cash flow and a $50 million (pro forma) profit (1989 results), they think "wow—look at those huge profits." But the reality is our net cash flow, after capital expenditures and corporate G&A was $160 million and our return on capital employed was 3%—well below our long-term cost of capital. These were not attractive returns from an investor's perspective, given that we have over $3 billion of capital employed in our operation. In addition, our operating margins were pretty thin in 1989 (about $4 Canadian per barrel), so we were very vulnerable to drops in world crude oil prices.

**VOICES**

We decided that as part of our goal of having all employees "thinking and acting like owners of the Company," employees needed to understand more than just production and costs—they needed to know the revenue side, margins, cash flow, and returns.

We established that if we could cut our operating costs from $18 (US) per barrel to $9 for 1995, we could generate healthy operating margins and an attractive 12% return on capital employed. At these levels, we pointed out to employees that our joint venture owners (and their shareholders) would be very interested in investing in the further growth of our company. We also showed how this growth would improve everyone's employment security and the prospects for further job growth and development. Additionally, we pointed out that employees would gain financially in two ways—through our employee gainshare ("IMPACT") program and through improved dividends and market share value of royalty trust units that many of our employees hold in two of our joint venture owner companies.

As it turns out, our 1995 results were a significant improvement over our position back in 1989. Operating costs were down to $10 (US) per barrel, operating cash flow increased to $614 million, and earnings (pro forma) were $265 million, generating an 8.9% return on capital employed. Due to this performance, employees earned a significant gainshare payout and the value of the royalty trusts units has grown substantially, especially in recent months, in 1996. All of this is helping to reinforce how good "bottom line" financial performance benefits all stakeholders, including employees."

- *OBM Can Help Meet Competitive Pressures.* Ideally when a company chooses to install open-book management practices in anticipation of increased competition, it does so before it's in the middle of scrambling to combat the threat. But even in the heat of battle, the institution of open-book management practices creates powerful response mechanisms to competition.

### ☑ SURVEY

Not surprisingly, many company presidents responding to our survey said that the biggest reason for adopting OBM was its timeliness and applicability to the emerging global competitive climate.

Mark Stewart, director of Human Resources for Schrock Cabinet Company in Dublin, Ohio, describes the changing environment to which his company is responding:

VOICES

"The Schrock Cabinet Company was formed two years ago from four separate, fairly autonomous units that as a whole had seen fairly good sales growth but unacceptable profitability. The cabinet industry is a mature one, so industry sales are expected to grow more slowly than with new products. The industry is now 73% remodeling, a large shift from the former emphasis on new construction. Huge home center chains like Home Depot and Lowes are replacing smaller stores: Fewer and bigger customers make a tougher environment for the cabinet industry. There is also little opportunity for innovation in materials and design, there are low entry and exit barriers to competitors, and competition is very fragmented with many small players. Given the market in which we compete, the difference between winning and losing is on-time and complete delivery and service to our customers, consistent quality, and low costs. The leadership of SCC believe that to compete effectively in our market, we must tap into the talents of all SCC associates, and open-book management is one tool to achieve this."

- *OBM Can Sharpen Customer Focus.* Companies that put the customer first require every individual to be thinking and acting for this common goal. Open-book management is the perfect way to encourage this behavior because it directly links customer satisfaction, employee goals, and overall company success. Perhaps the single best example of what open-book practices can do to sharpen customer focus is MANCO, a $145 million producer of duct tape based in Cleveland. Its employees absolutely believe—and have seen demonstrated—that if they want to make more money they have to help their *customers* make more money. Here's how one employee puts it:

"We can't win if our customers don't win. Wal-Mart and Kmart are very important to us, but so are the little companies. What we've learned is that when our customers ask us for more, they are asking us to take on additional cost. But if we do it right, it's not an additional cost, it's additional value."

**VOICES**

Manco is the open-book management company you have to see to believe, a sort of no-kidding ownership motivational masterpiece. You will read more about its systems and impressive results in Chapter 6.

- *OBM Can Help Start-Ups, Acquisitions, or New Divisions Get Off on the Right Foot.* The blank slate of a start-up company offers the perfect chance to inculcate open-book values right from the beginning. Results can be impressive when a gain-sharing program is aimed at the first-year business plan, when education about the industry and the market opportunity is detailed in the strategic plan, when a business, from day one, institutes focused huddles to compare actual results with those projected in the company's pro forma income statement.

Whole Foods Market in Austin, Texas, started in 1982 and was founded on open-book principles. By

1984 they had their initial gain-sharing plans, and two years later opened the books in detail. When they went public in 1992, their open-book foundation was already deep. Now Whole Foods has 69 stores and 10,000 employees generating over $1.2 billion in revenue. CEO John Mackey uses open-book practices as a core system for empowering the team-based structure that is at the heart of all Whole Foods stores:

**VOICES**

"We empower our employees by putting them in teams and sharing the responsibilities and the rewards. If the teams come in under their labor budget, they start getting the bonus. Every store we purchase comes into the same system."

Having started gain-sharing in 1984, and more open-book practices in 1987, including an open salary process, their culture was solidly business literate by the time they began to purchase their many new stores in the 1990s.

## How Does OBM Change People's Behavior—and Get Results?

The most useful resource that companies have is the thinking capacity of its people applied to its goals. What happens to people in an open-book company can be the most challenging yet satisfying aspect of OBM. Tim O'Donnell from *Olathe Daily News* was amazed at the magnified effectiveness brought about by his business-literate culture:

**VOICES**

"You couldn't have told me that we were going to become profitable by expense management. I thought we had to grow revenues. But when all the managers understood that they could actually have an impact on profitability, they found the improvements in savings. I don't think I could have seen those potential savings from my position."

With all players informed about their business and its financial goals, they play on a level field, speak a common language, and are focused on a common outcome. This leads to a natural improvement in employee's esteem, concentration, and thinking. People at different levels acknowledge, utilize, and respect the contribution of others. Managers learn to evaluate new product lines or new projects for their economic value added to the overall business goals. Power and information are more easily shared with a common understanding of both goals and roles.

## How Does OBM Make This Happen?

- *It Aligns Day-to-Day Priorities with Business Goals.* Open-book management practices challenge everyone in the organization to look at and assess their actions and responsibilities in relationship to their effect on the business results. And this is not just an annual or semiannual or quarterly event. This is a way of thinking, a way of ordering one's daily priorities.

In open-book companies individuals learn to see how they fit into the overall business dynamic and to understand the implications of what they are seeing. This allows them to comprehend their contribution differently and to set priorities in a clear-headed, goal-driven way, not out of a knee-jerk response to the pressure cooker of day-to-day stresses.

Consequently, managers learn to delegate more. They trust that employees know enough to make decisions with an eye on the business, not just on the task at hand. A sales professional, for instance, with guidance and teaching from an open-book management leader, can decide to shift her sales goals from pure volume to profitable sales to better align her results with the company's target numbers.

Work in open-book companies is fast paced, but people can respond intelligently to the real pressure cooker, not to make-believe ones. Because an OBM environment focuses people, it has a positive effect on their understanding, well-being and, ultimately, the company's success.

- *It Diminishes Politics.* In traditional "political" environments, a lot of energy is wasted on building fiefdoms by excluding others from key information. These are not goals of the business, but needs of individuals to control and build power. Those needs, focused on the wrong outcomes, can often be destructive to the business. Pleasing the boss is part of misused power. It is deeply entrenched in most companies because it has been a requirement in traditional management for years. Job descriptions spell out support of the bosses' position. In many cases, the translation becomes an unspoken norm and expectation to make the boss look good. Supervisors and managers confined to pleasing a boss soon learn that it doesn't pay for them to think independently, to strategize, to question what is good for the business. The "political necessities" become the focus of thinking and behaving.

Open-book management practices tend to override political networks because, with OBM, power is aimed at business results not individual gains. Bosses learn to love questions. It is in their best interests to be part of a thinking team. After all, the boss's performance and reward—as well as the team's—is predicted on everyone's ability to act knowledgeably based on timely, accurate, complete information.

Looking good for the boss is just as important in open-book companies as in any traditional company. But looking good in an OBM environment doesn't mean withholding information and avoiding political mistakes. Indeed, how good you look in an OBM company is based on how much you learn, and that often involves making mistakes, and sharing the new information to move ahead.

- *It Redefines and Redistributes Power.* The power in an open-book management company then, does not so much reside in people as in the *connections* made between people and the quality of the information that passes through those connections. Once the business's goals are commonly known by all, those connections can produce powerful results.

This does not mean that all positions have equal power however. Hierarchy remains and positions with more responsibility and risk are valued with higher compensation. What is different in open-book companies is that the people in senior positions no longer withhold information or delude themselves that they are the only ones who can think about and understand the business challenges and financial goals.

For this to happen, there must be a shift in the perspective of the people occupying the senior positions. Rather than using their power to distance themselves, they must come to see themselves as educators and co-ordinators of effort and information flow. They must use their influence and knowledge to help others as well as themselves achieve results, to develop a sense of team.

Leaders in open-book management companies enthusiastically pursue the development and utilization of all employees' brains, hearts, and hands. The CFO of a medium-sized growth company, for example, came to the second day of an open-book management workshop for managers and operations directors an hour early. He did the teaching himself, walked everyone through the company's financial statements, gave examples, answered and asked questions. Then he joined the training group for an informal lunch. The participants raved about the information they gained about their business: "It is so much clearer to me now why we are so focused on call-handling time. I can see the financial implications," says one. The result of this understanding was made clear, as call-handling time was tracked thereafter and showed a significant and measurable reduction.

When the CFO not only taught facts, but also socialized and connected with people, he created the emotional climate for learning that, when combined with knowledge and information, makes teamwork powerful and effective. The single most influential factor, then, in integrating OBM practices and philosophy into the day-to-day life of a company is the *observable actions* of those in positions of power. The company's leaders must be involved and visible to send and continuously reinforce the open-book message. Derrick Kershaw, a general manager in Operations, describes how that happens at Syncrude:

**VOICES**

"Our approach to moving from traditional power-over structures to power-within-the-employee teams is based on knowing and acting on key performance factors. We have not given up control of the business—we've vested it in more of our people and as they have taken control and ownership of their work and their results we see superior performance and business results. To enable these shifts in the way the business is run required that the senior people in the company communicate a very clear, simple vision of what the business is, where it is going, and where it could go. Also, the values that we will all use as we work with each other internally and as we work with our customers and suppliers. Company policies and procedures have to be modified either proactively or in response to changes in the way the work is being managed."

Kershaw's statement points out the critical role a company's culture plays in how effectively it can apply open-book principles. Are your company's mission and core beliefs consistent with open-book philosophy?

In the next chapter, we will provide the operating principles behind OBM that will help you answer this question.

# 2

## The Business Context for OBM

### OBM: The Key Operating Principles

*The facts are that the coming decades will bring more, not less, competition and more, not less, challenge. Organizations which attempt to meet these competitors and challengers with one hand tied behind their back as a result of keeping their employees from becoming total team members, face the prospect of real failure. A diverse and motivated workforce which is connected and knowledgeable about the company they are involved in will provide that management team with the kind of global edge which could separate dramatic success from slow atrophy. The use of open-book management to unite and empower that diverse workforce of the future is perhaps its greatest promise.\**

Chris Kuehl, PhD
Economist
The Global Group

A decade of downsizings, mergers, and deregulation has brought the marketplace into every business. Beyond every cubicle or workstation is a customer with choices, and employees who were relegated to carrying out management's orders in the old bureaucratic days, are now being asked to make customers happy with new and better solutions and to improve the bottom line while they are at it. Employees

---

\* The entire essay from which this excerpt is taken is reprinted in Appendix III.

who once were able to just show up for jobs now have to make the business grow.

Before open-book management, departmental measures of success, born of bureaucratic budgets, were most often the focus. One division's gain was another's loss. Open-book management requires employees to be business-literate and accountable. That creates companywide, not departmental, focus. It engenders flexibility, teamwork, and responsiveness and, ultimately, a healthy balance sheet.

In many companies, employees now share equally with management the responsibility for quality, service, innovation, and financial health (Figure 2–1). Management systems that do not tap the intelligence of *all* their workers are simply not capable of standing up to the challenge. And when these systems are in place, a number of key operating principles emerge.

- *Think and Act Systemically.* When we talk about an "organization," what is organized is a number of different types of resources or "parts"—people, equipment, space, information, knowledge, and money. They are organized for a purpose that can often be forgotten when the parts, especially the people, start interacting and interfacing with one another. Agendas can develop that have little or nothing to do with the overall goals of the organization.

| 1950s/1960s | 1970s | 1980s | 1990s | 2000 |
|---|---|---|---|---|
| Research into Participative Management Begins in Earnest | | Widespread Involvement of Employees in Teams and Quality | | Widespread Involvement of Employees as Business Thinkers and Partners |
| | Introduce Participative Management Philosophy | | Introduce Open-Book Philosophy and Practices | |

**Figure 2–1.** Employees share responsibility.

Open-book management aligns the functions of all parts of an enterprise. The three most important relationships in an open-book company are: (1) The relationship between the individual and the business goals of the company. This requires that each person have a direct line of sight between his or her daily tasks and the performance of the company as measured by key indicators; (2) the relationship between the individual and the system or function he or she directly influences; and (3) the relationship between the individual and his or her team members.

## BUSINESS FOCUS

The point of reference for daily decision making is the current performance of the company to its business plan targets. The amount of time spent on various activities may shift in order to achieve expected outcomes. The short-term focus to deliver needed results is modulated by the knowledge of long-term objectives. Employees weigh risks against the short- and long-term business goals every day throughout the company.

Every person in the organization as well as those on the outside, namely customers and suppliers, have thoughts, ideas, and a set of experiences that provides a continuous source of information and feedback for employees to utilize when making decisions or noticing problems and opportunities. Once most employees know and understand the business in a specific and *personal* way, a unifying picture emerges.

- *Harness Intellectual Capital.* One of the underlying objectives of the open-book management practices is to structure the communication and data flow and analysis in such a way as to trigger fresh perspectives on what could otherwise be considered the same old stuff. As individuals and teams compare their activities and results to their needed contribution to the big picture, they test their perception of what is happening. This prevents individual spins, assumptions, and perspectives from prevailing over a more complete set of data and helps to harness the company's intelligence.

- *Team Play.* As most of us have experienced, there is a limit to expertise. So open-book management practice demands the practice of partnering and collaborating to achieve the desired results. When employees are truly business literate, they understand the mechanisms by which the organization can succeed. When they understand their role in creating that success and their potential reward that can be engendered by that success, team work is reinforced by a keen awareness of cause-and-effect linkage between functions.

- *Relentless Intentional Learning.* In stark contrast to the command-and-control model, business literate environments are information rich. Through intentional learning, employees make positive use of the mistakes that individual players make everyday in companies. In the traditional management approach, individuals work in overdrive to hide and cover up their mistakes and their ignorance for fear of embarrassment and punishing consequences. In open-book management, a realistic view is taken that mistakes happen, but recognizing and correcting them quickly is a key to competitive advantage. Mistakes are recognized and corrected most quickly in communicative and information-rich environments.

- *Accountability.* Every person accounts to their teammates in the company about the effectiveness of their contribution. This accounting includes both aspects of the results that the person has control over and those they do not. For example, as a customer service team leader accounts for his or her team's overtime hours that exceeded budget by $5000 for the month the information may include an unexpected illness or an increase in service demand that the team hadn't forecasted accurately. The team leader is expected to manage what is controllable as well as the surprises in a way that the budgeted results are achieved. The team knows and accepts the challenge of getting back to the planned performance. They know it is their responsibility to problem-solve ways to make up for the negative variance. Similarly, the CEO accounts to the stockholders or investors.

The full picture, the whole story, the play-by-play account drives a *results-oriented* culture. Coupled with the continuous learning principle, employees remain motivated to perform and inform at a high and intense level.

- *A Stake in the Outcome for All.* In open-book management, each employee should be tied, in part, to the business's overall financial goals (like profitability or economic value added) and in part to the performance drivers that he or she can actually affect (purchase prices, market share, sales or training costs). The common linkage to the financial outcome becomes a unifying motivator for all. There is also a corresponding risk for all. Open-book management develops collective awareness of the difficult challenges involved in running a business. Employees gain an appreciation of the good, the bad, and the uncontrollably ugly. Being able to bounce back from setbacks is an important capability in any business. In those businesses managed by open-book management, the players accept this fact, take responsibility for

their own disappointments and contributions toward to the outcomes, and prepare themselves to
"play another season."

- *Recognition and Celebration.* For all the mistakes
that must be acknowledged, accepted, and corrected an equally important principle in open-
book management is to recognize and celebrate
achievements and achievers. When participants
experience themselves as part of the risk, they
gain a genuine sense of fulfillment when the goal
is achieved. With OBM, each person is part of the
business story. It is these stories that make the
numbers interesting that in turn provide emotional, psychological, and financial satisfaction.

- *Ethical Behavior.* This is both a necessary ingredient and an inevitable by-product of open-book
management. An ingredient because a company
of business-literate people who align themselves
toward a goal of profit at all costs will corrupt itself and ultimately fail. A by-product because
open information, open accountability, and open
setting of goals creates an environment in which
unethical behavior cannot thrive.

- *Leadership.* All the previous principles are intimately tied to the leadership. As we described
in *The Power of Open-Book Management,* leadership is *the* most important factor in sustaining
the open-book practices and therefore for the
achievement of the business results year after
year. In open-book management companies, the
responsibility and authority for operational,
sales, and financial decisions are pushed down
the hierarchical ladder, leaving company leaders
the primary tasks of mentoring, teaching, coaching, developing, providing direction, informing,
guiding, and communicating. This is the catalyst that sparks the open-book engine and keeps
it running optimally.

| Principle | Definition | What Are People Thinking | What Are People Doing | Required Level of Competence |
|---|---|---|---|---|
| Think and act systematically | The perspective of an organization as a system of interconnected interdependent parts. | About the other functional parts that they influence with specific decisions or actions. | Communicate with people in other positions to get input; inform others of reasons behind proposed decisions or actions. | High |
| | | About the impact of a decision or action has on the company's short- and long-term goals. | Calculate and/or discuss the big-picture implications of proposed decision/action. | |
| | | About the whole task, of which they are a part. | When appropriate communicate and link with others for efficiency and effectiveness of decision/action. | |
| Business focus | The point of reference for daily decision making, judgment calls, and priorities. | Primarily about the current year's goals and the critical performance drivers; people in highest positions think more about long-term objectives and the primary purpose of the business. | Review and or study current and forecasted performance and financial statements. Analyze variances to determine priorities; senior leaders communicate the purpose of the business as the frame of reference and focus. | Medium to high |
| Harness all intellectual capital | The utilization of the many sources of business information. | Weigh risks/ rewards of decisions and actions. | Communicate, as appropriate, to others the assessed risk, current perspective of expected threats and opportunities. | |
| | | About who can shed light on problems and opportunities. | Contract and solicit input from those who can be useful; assess the implications of action if appropriate. | Low to medium |
| | | About who would most likely have a different experience or perspective than ones own. | Ask questions and listen to those whose view of the problem or opportunity is different; explore underlying common goal; determine best action. | |
| Team play | A tight coordination of all employees calibrated to achievement of business goals. | About themselves as a participant on a team. | Staying in contact with teammates; seeks information to see a complete picture. | Medium to high |
| | | About how teamwork can best be carried out and his/her role in the work processes. | Planning, deciding, acting in coordination so the key business goals can be reached. | |
| | | About subordinating teams needs, if necessary, to reach the goal of the whole business. | | |
| Relentless intentional learning | Individual and team pursuit of business knowledge and putting the knowledge into wise action. | About what knowledge they lack; what understanding is fuzzy or incomplete. | Seeking and obtaining the knowledge needed from appropriate internal or external sources; asking questions and listening to deeper understanding. | Medium to high |
| | | About what knowledge and/or understanding they have that others might need. | Contacting the internal or external business associates to provide information that could be of use, increase understanding or alter a perspective. | |

*(continued)*

**Figure 2–2.** Principles of open-book management.

| Principle | Definition | What Are People Thinking | What Are People Doing | Required Level of Competence |
|---|---|---|---|---|
| Accountability | Each person owns a defined output and accounts for the status of the output on a regular and consistant basis. | About the other team members that are counting on them for a defined outcome. | Communicates and updates others quickly on charges. | Low to medium |
| | | About the importance of accounting for their performance status accurately and completely. | Analyzes the current status within sphere of responsibility. Communicates the analysis with supporting evidence; explores possible alterations and communicates to appropriate teammates. | |
| Stake in the outcome for all | Each employee's financial compensation and emotional satisfaction is, in part, tied to their company's business results. | About themselves as a valuable and needed contributor to the business. | Assigns weighted value on their decision making; prioritizes and allocates time and other resources based on knowledge of their position's contribution. | Medium to high |
| | | About the importance for the business to achieve its business objectives. | Goes beyond own personal interest to assist others, to inform and teach others keeping the business objectives in mind. | |
| | | About the psychic and financial pay-offs for the committed effort. | Do anything they can to assure company goals and pay-out levels are reached. | |
| Recognition and celebration | Frequently recognizing and celebrating the individual and team contributors to achieving a goal, overcoming an obstacle, or meeting a challenge. | About who is contributing currently, in a significant way, to the ongoing business. | Setting a specific time to recognize the individual(s). | Low to high |
| | | About a way to recognize those involved that celebrates the people. | Makes an outline of key things to publicly and/or privately praise. | |
| | | About using recognition as a way of teaching what is valuable. | Repeatedly tells stories about others achievements in the business. | |
| | | | Encourages others to learn from those being recognized. | |
| Ethical behavior | Obedience to a set of otherwise unenforceable behavioral standards that respects the rights of others. | About the consequences of one's decisions and actions; about the favorable or unfavorable impact of one's behavior on others. | Discussing awareness of both positive and negative consequences with others in the company. | High |
| | | About the needs of the larger community of which the business is a part. | Questioning behavior that appears to unfavorably impact others. | |
| | | | Making decisions form a set of thoughtful principles that one is proud to be known for. | |
| | | | Providing a role model for others on making "tough but right" choices. | |

*(continued)*

**Figure 2–2.** *(Continued)*

| Principle | Definition | What Are People Thinking | What Are People Doing | Required Level of Competence |
|---|---|---|---|---|
| Leadership | Taking the lead, breaking new ground, assuming risk and appropriate responsibility to assist the company in reaching its goals. | About what strategy is currently needed to sustain business success. | Discussing observations and strategies with others; taking a lead to initiate action. | High |
| | | About where coaching and teaching is needed. | Offering guidance, information and explanation. | |
| | | About one's own learning needs. | Seeking out others perspectives, maintain industry knowledge. | |
| | | About how to strengthen communication linkages throughout the company. | Routinely survey employee awareness and knowledge level of the business needs. | |

**Figure 2–2.** *(Continued)*

Figure 2–2 summarizes how each of these core OBM principles plays out in the day-to-day thoughts and actions of employees. It is a graphic representation of the cohesive, results-oriented kind of enterprise OBM creates as well as the level of competence needed to sustain it.

In the next chapter, we'll help you assess whether the climate in your company is favorable to OBM, and what steps you'll need to take to prepare to go open-book.

# 3

# *Creating the OBM Climate*

## How to Assess Your Company's Readiness and Prepare to Go Open-Book

*We began at the business staff level (direct reports to the president) by forming a core team that began studying OBM and proposed a course of action in mid-1995. We ran a pilot process with all our business staff and operating team leadership. Based upon feedback from the pilots, we established a team of champions to plan our OBM initiatives. This team met in late 1995 and developed a plan for OBM throughout the business, including top level commitment, education plan, and all supporting efforts to interweave OBM into our business. The team met in person and via video-conference, and subteams took responsibility for components such as education and training. We conducted a survey of leadership, business, and financial knowledge so we would have a baseline that we used to assess training needs and track our progress against. We wanted to do all this seamlessly, without making it look or feel like a "program."*

Mark Stewart
Director of Human Resources
Schrock Cabinet Company
Dublin, Ohio

In order to evaluate your company's readiness for business literacy it is useful to know in advance what the full development cycle looks like, from preparation and planning to implementation, operation, and continual improvement. Projecting the resources needed and the pacing of the learning effort will come from a planned approach (Figure 3–1).

**GETTING IT STARTED**

| Phases | Objectives | Participants | Activities | Resources Needed | Time Required | Common Pitfalls |
|---|---|---|---|---|---|---|
| 1.A. Awareness (Chapter 7) | Comprehend OBM and what it offers | Senior Managers | Read articles and books Visit practitioners On-site briefing | OBM* literature OBM coach | 4–6 hours 1–2 days | Sound simple Easy to "tell" vs. providing leadership |
| 1.B. Determine Level of Readiness (Chapter 7) | Assess current levels of competency | Task force OBM consultant | Survey Interviews | Set of standard practices Coordination and planning | Over course of 1–2 months | Seen as unimportant Rushed Too small a sample in data gathering |
| 2. Define Goals (Chapter 7) | Articulate direction for company with OBM Specify goals —Critical Numbers —No-Kidding Ownership —Huddle System —Leadership Practice | Senior Managers with input from those involved in Phase I task force | Workshop Think Tank Review and analyze data of the Readiness report Designate Design Team members | OBM facilitator Readiness report Strategic and business plans Evaluation of current initiatives | 1–2 day workshop Individual preparation time: approx. 2 hours | Lack of individual preparation and buy-in Turf and politics Minimal big-picture thinking |
| 3. Establish and Educate the Team Implementation (Chapter 8) | Deep learning Identify best connections for linking OBM to current company strengths and goals | Implementation Team —Mid-Managers —Functional experts | OBM training Study OBM materials Share learning Site visits to OBM companies Trial applications Identify barriers | Meeting time OBM materials OBM coach Direction from senior management | Weekly learning and application meetings for 1–2 months Individual reading/study | Canceled meetings Unprepared team members Overwhelmed by other demands Lack of management support |

**KEEPING IT GOING**

| Phases | Objectives | Participants | Activities | Resources Needed | Time Required | Common Pitfalls |
|---|---|---|---|---|---|---|
| 4.A. Crafting the plan (Chapter 9) | Craft implementation plan | Implementation Team Sub-teams design bows and Huddle System | Planning Workshop Set Milestones | Workshop facilitator Readiness report from Phase II | 1–2 day workshop Subteam meeting time | Lack of leadership support Failure to reschedule canceled meetings |
| 4.B. Design and Conduct Training (Chapter 10) | Develop and pilot basic OBM and Critical Numbers training | Sub-teams to develop specific training components | Recruit sub-teams Gather resources Develop and write training Initiate training | Employees with financial and business knowhow OBM coach and trainer | 6–10 development and planing sessions Schedule for training | Lack of training resources |
| 5. Implementation and Rollout (Introduction to Section III) (Chapters 12, 13, 14) | Initiate use of OBM practices through the company Reinforce business thinking and real time education in Huddle System | All managers and employees of the company | Create or refine scorecards Start huddles and practices Flag opportunities for learning Celebrate small victories Coach huddle leaders Conduct training Align reward/bonus program | Scorecards Current data on customers, operations, etc. Managers who coach and run huddles | Weekly Huddles 40-minute pre-huddle 60–90-minute main huddle 30-minute post-huddle Continue basic business finance classes | Form over substance in huddles Impatience for perfection Missing opportunities Bonus not working Impatience |
| 6. Ongoing Improvement (Chapters 12, 13, 14) | Improve business results by mastering OBM practices | All in the company | Ongoing huddles Frequent recognition Develop new leaders | Semiannual evaluation by design team | Time enough to continue the learning and educating | Lack of consistent accountability Lack of vision |

**Figure 3–1.** The six implementation phases of OBM.

The first level—Awareness/Determining Your Company's Level of Readiness—is critical to success. The more thoughtfully and thoroughly a company *prepares* itself for its open-book management journey the fewer pitfalls and setbacks it is likely to encounter along the way. This requires vision and commitment on the part of the leadership. John Mackey, CEO of Whole Foods Market, identifies one of the first implementation steps as "know thyself before you go open-book." John believes this includes an analysis of your history, your culture (climate), your critical values, and your company's financial situation. The investigation into these areas lays the groundwork for OBM.

When thinking through the preparation of your company's internal climate you have to look at the application and benefits of open-book management in the context of other initiatives already at work in your organization. Many companies find it useful to connect open-book to current initiatives and other organizational strengths. That way you are not only building on an existing culture, but you create direct procedural and philosophical linkages with existing processes.

The initiatives that open-book connects quite naturally with are team-based organizational structures, total quality management, re-engineering, employee participation programs, employee empowerment programs, whole task redesign, and customer satisfaction programs. In some organizations, as Mark Stewart describes in the opening quote, the linkages can be made so seamlessly that open-book management doesn't even need to be named as a new initiative or program—just an extension of or a comprehensive approach to existing ones.

In other cases, naming it and framing it gets the attention of employees and provides the context and rationale for the shift and changes that happen with open-book management. As Cathy Kramer, executive director of the Association for Quality and Participation (AQP) puts it, "Open-book management is both a cause and a manifestation of effective workplaces. It fits because it sets the context."

Don de Guerre, manager of organizational effectiveness at Syncrude Canada, Ltd., helped his organization think through the advantages and "make sense" linkages:

**VOICES**

"When Business Literacy (or open-book management) was introduced as the third phase of redesign it was a natural fit. It was introduced to the company as a new paradigm—a different way of thinking about a reliable statistical methodology that could guide the daily business decisions of all employees. The notion of an intensive huddle system using scorecards provided a renewed impetus to make our stewardship system work. Each team developed a line of sight to company business results such that every employee understood their contribution to Syncrude's critical numbers. Open-book management reasserts a way for managers and leaders to work in teams to monitor critical numbers and intervene only when safety, reliability, or profitability were in jeopardy. Thus our redesign process, active at middle-management levels of the company, has a new common sense about how to describe the middle's work in a new form of work organization. We continue to explore ways to link compensation and rewards more directly to business results. OBM is a good conceptual framework that clearly rewards business."

## Assessing Where You Stand

Whether or not you plan to bill the introduction of OBM as something new, you'll need to gauge what it will take to create or reinforce the culture OBM requires. Here are several approaches you can use as a guide to get a relatively quick snapshot of where your company stands.

**How Ready Is Your Management Team?**  Your first step should be to hold informal discussions one-on-one with each of your team members. Remember, if you are the boss, it's unfortunate but true that people usually tell you what they think you want to hear. Without tipping your hand about your interest in OBM, you are going to have to do some homework and get real answers to the following:

- Do we have a good understanding of what OBM is and what it will entail?
- What business targets should OBM help us hit?
- What kind of problems do we want it to solve?
- How will we apply the principles to our particular culture?
- What kind of preparation will we need to do?
- How ready are we to teach employees everything we know about our business?

Perhaps the best follow-up to your informal discussions is an offsite meeting facilitated by an OBM consultant during which people feel relaxed, free to speak their minds, and unhurried to reach a conclusion. This is an important step in the life of your company, so *don't rush it.* You may decide that an open-book strategy makes sense in light of your business goals and your culture, or you may decide to postpone any OBM initiatives until certain short-term goals are met. There are no wrong answers, but you must ask the questions before you move ahead.

It would be unusual if every senior manager was equally enthused about moving ahead with an OBM approach to running the business. If that seems to be happening, think again! Ask yourself what you haven't thought of. Ask what barriers and other types of resistance there could be. Consider which individuals or departments might have something to lose. For example, if the sales group is used to getting all the attention, are they prepared to share the glory (or the heat)? Conversely, are other departments ready to have the spotlight turned on them?

It is healthy to have managers asking "What if" or "What about." Listen to them and think through the implications of their concerns. Determine how you will manage resistance and who can help you minimize negativity.

In our experience, there are very few companies that have the ideal setting and culture to gracefully and easily accept open-book practices. So it can be extremely useful for each department head to identify, in advance, the adjustments his or her employees will likely need to make. Ultimately, it will be the strength of your belief in OBM, and that of the manager-mentors in the company, that will sustain the open-book transformation when inevitable bumps in the road are encountered.

**What Is the Level of Business Coaching Competency at Your Company?** Circulate a survey among your team leaders, middle managers, and senior managers. Use Figure 3–2 as a guide. The survey results will show your strengths and weaknesses. Use it as a basis for creating a program to build a management team of business coaches. Develop an assessment of each manager's business coaching competency. Set standards of demonstrated business coaching competency and begin to formally and informally train the leaders in your company to meet them. Once you have identified your strong business coaches, you can establish a mentoring system to help develop others. As we describe in other chapters, those in leadership roles at your company will be the linchpins of your open-book success. Make sure they are set up to succeed themselves.

_____          _____
      Department                              Position

1. How often do you use the company's financial statements as a point of reference when explaining something about the business?

2. How frequently do you seize a "teachable moment" to explain to your team some aspect of the business? Please give an example:

3. How often do you conduct business education meetings with your team? Provide examples of topics you covered recently.

4. How do you personally continue your learning about our business?

**Figure 3–2.** Business coach leadership survey.

**Do Your Employees Understand Business Finance?**
Figure 3–3 is a quick and revealing survey to gauge financial literacy in your organization. We created it for the Association for Quality and Participation's 1994 Conference. Since then it has been referenced in *BusinessWeek* and has also been employed by a number of university professors as well as by companies who

T   F   A bankrupt company can be profitable.
T   F   In business, profit is the same as cash.
T   F   Under general accounting principles, accounts receivable are not counted as an asset until actually collected.
T   F   A company can operate without cash.
T   F   An income statement shows whether a company is operating profitably.

1. The solvency of a company is related to:
   a. How much cash it has on hand.
   b. Its ratio of debt to equity.
   c. Its margin of profitability.

2. A company's net worth is equal to:
   a. Its total revenue minus expenses and debt.
   b. Its fair market price.
   c. Its total assets minus its total liabilities.

3. A company's equity is another name for its:
   a. Net worth.
   b. Combined value.
   c. Total assets.

4. A company's profitability percentage is determined by dividing:
   a. Gross sales revenues by net sales revenues.
   b. Net income by total sales revenues.
   c. The company's net worth by the difference between its assets and liabilities.

5. COGS is an acronym for:
   a. Common Operating Guidelines and Standards.
   b. Cost of Goods Sold.
   c. Credibility of Given Statistics.

**Figure 3–3.** What's your BLQ (Business Literacy Quotient)? (See Appendix IV for answers.)

want a quick gauge of their employees' knowledge. The questions can and should be modified to fit your company's business.

Some companies use this BLQ as a way to raise awareness of their employees' lack of business literacy. Often it's used as the precursor to offering a series of business education classes and then as a measure of progress after the classes are completed.

If the scores are low, which often they are, you can plan on using your training resources for the next year or two to educate your workforce. Then, even after employees have been educated with the basics, the communication and accountability system we call *intensive huddle* is necessary to provide regular opportunities for all contributors to use and improve their know-how.

**Establish Specific Competency Levels of Financial Understanding.** Setting up learning targets lets your employees and managers know what you expect. It also helps to develop an intense business-learning environment. Determine the different target levels of competency needed for different groups at your company such as managers, line workers, salespeople, and make clear who you expect to attain what level and why. These gradations of financial literacy will be both goals in themselves and, a way to together, map out the learning journey on which employees can embark. They also provide milestones by which you can continually measure your company's progress. Here are some samples of different levels:

- *Level One: Basic.* All employees can read the company's income statement and distinguish revenues, expenses, profit and loss; all employees can calculate the company's profit margin, explain the difference between profit and cash, and name the company's main financial goals.

- *Level Two: Intermediate.* All employees can read the company's balance sheet and distinguish assets, liabilities, and net worth; all employees can name and calculate the company's key financial ratios. Manager can explain the company's equity and department positions and ROE or other ratios.
- *Level Three: Advanced.* All managers and some employees can explain and *educate others* about the company's complete short-term financial condition; all managers and some employees can provide a comprehensive description of the company's long-term financial needs and can explain the business's finance activities, such as loans and investments.

**Do Your Employees Use Financial Information to Make Decisions?**   At your next budget review meeting, have the CFO or budget officer ask some simple questions:

- How often have managers shared the information on monthly variance reports to help you and your team make decisions?
- How often have employees seen the budget or the financial variance report? Did the reports improve performance?
- How can financial information be used in the future to improve the quality and timeliness of decisions?

At the same time, send out a financial survey to all employees asking questions like:

- Have you seen the strategic and operating plan? If yes, how often do you use this information in decision making?

- Do you see the company's monthly and quarterly results?
- How often do you use financial information in your day-to-day work? What numbers do you most often employ in doing so?
- How often do you use financial information when considering customer requests?
- How often do you use financial information when evaluating projects with teammates?
- What don't you understand about the financial aspects of your business?

One company we worked with sent out this type of survey and was stunned by the results. The top people couldn't believe how many managers and director-level employees—many of whom had MBAs—were not using financial information and/or were working from outdated numbers and assumptions. They moved quickly to put a plan together to address their problems: poor communication, unclear expectations, and an outdated reporting system.

Each company will have unique issues to deal with but several categories of problems tend to show up again and again:

- Communication hand-offs either don't happen, are not timely, or are inaccurate.
- The wrong things are being measured.
- Needed information for smart business decisions arrives too late.
- Different people have different definitions of business concepts like gross margin, economic value added, cash on hand, or even profit, and different understandings of what they mean to the company.
- Many see the responsibility for knowing critical business measures and taking action to improve them as someone else's job.

Open-book practices help correct these problems through business education, reinforced by ongoing intensive huddles and continuous player-coach leadership.

**How Effective Is Your Bonus System?**   No-Kidding Ownership is a foundational element for any open-book initiative. If people don't really feel they have a stake in the company, and that they can directly *affect* that stake, then other open-book practices have little leverage. You may already have some sort of variable compensation program, probably a bonus system. But is it working? Is it motivating people to excel? You need to ask all employees the following questions:

- What is the purpose of the company incentive plan?
- What target(s) is the bonus tied to? Do individuals or teams have different targets or are they working at cross purposes?
- Do you feel the plan is fair?
- Does your bonus provide you with incentive? How so?
- Should you get your bonus if you work hard, but the company does not meet its financial goals?

If the answers indicate your bonus plan is less than effective, it would be wise to create a bonus design team from a cross-section of employees to delve more deeply into how to create incentive compensation that works. This team can explore and adapt the incentive structures of any number of companies—many of which are mentioned in this book—that have designed creative plans to drive very specific business results.

Make a serious commitment to this. Provide a budget. Be prepared to hire external experts if a new bonus approach seems necessary. And don't do any of this if you aren't prepared to follow through.

## Start an Education Program

Once you have a good sense of where your company stands on the road to open-book, you'll need to begin the education process that will get you there. An education program that teaches financial principles or business principles stretches people to learn and apply at the same time.

In Section Two of this book, we detail how several successful open-book companies use educational tools and programs to teach all employees to think in the common language of business. If you want to get a head start, without a lot of preparation, here are some tried-and-true educational tactics:

**Create Scorecards.** Scorecards are useful tools. They track the progress of a department, team, or individual toward meeting a specific outcome. The visibility of a scorecard focuses individuals on the factors that lead to desired outcomes and stimulates the learning process. Figures 3–4 and 3–5 show samples of simple scorecards that can serve as a stimulus for business learning. Chapter 6 describes more advanced scorecarding applications.

Goal:

| Individual Contribution | Weeks | | | | Monthly Total | Monthly Target |
|---|---|---|---|---|---|---|
| | 1 | 2 | 3 | 4 | | |
| Mary | | | | | | |
| Joe | | | | | | |
| Carla | | | | | | |
| Henry | | | | | | |

**Figure 3–4.** Monthly sales scoreboard.

Goal:

| Routes | Weeks | | | | Total |
|---|---|---|---|---|---|
| | 1 | 2 | 3 | 4 | |
| I. Mike's Team | | | | | |
| II. Linda's Team | | | | | |
| III. Tom's Team | | | | | |
| IV. Pat's Team | | | | | |
| $$ Saved | | | | | |

**Figure 3–5.** On-time deliveries scoreboard.

**Set a Clear Target.** The best way to begin to cultivate open-book thinking is to begin with relatively few unambiguously defined tasks with easily measured outcomes. For example, you might choose to try to lower departmental expenses, focusing on items that most team members have some control over. The combination of education and application focused on a straightforward target is a powerful learning device. It raises questions, illustrates tactics, and reveals knowledge gaps that you can then address.

**Be Experiential.** To provide a learning opportunity tailored to a specific business need, you can use case studies and customized business board games (more on this in Chapter 5). The experiential approach stimulates thinking and creative ideas. In experiences designed to create a positive environment, participants ask questions about the business that they won't feel comfortable asking in a typical one-on-one manager's meeting or in a staff meeting. The learning is quick, fun, and, with the right design for application, results can be achieved within a reasonable time frame.

Keep in mind as you work with the open-book practices and principles that you are on a learning journey. As a group, you'll need to constantly test your assumptions and revalidate your perspective. The learning, in a sense, never stops.

The next chapter is an ounce of preventive medicine to save a pound of painful open-book implementation cures. As the last chapter in the preparation section, it describes common pitfalls in OBM implementation and provides approaches and tips to avoid them entirely or pull yourself out of the hole if you are already there.

# 4

## Pitfalls and Paradoxes

### Common OBM Sticking Points and How to Negotiate Them

Practitioners of OBM, once they get past the "honeymoon" stage, inevitably reach at least one point where they say "Yes, but . . ." or "What happens when . . ." or "It can't work because . . ." Open-book management is such a fundamentally different way of thinking and acting that the implementation predictably runs into pitfalls.

Table 4–1 shows responses when respondents were asked to check the two items that they believe are the greatest obstacles to OBM implementation. Lack of follow-through (the #2 pitfall) can hurt any change effort. The #1 and #3 pitfalls, insufficient financial education and poor reward systems are more specific to OBM. (See Box on page 51.)

Many obstacles are natural sticking points and can be worked through over time if there is definable accountability, some measure of operational autonomy and budget control, and focused, mature leaders. Even if there are major obstacles, value can be gained from use of open-book management practices. Where limits and constraints exist, the practices can be partially applied and small gains can be achieved. For example,

**Table 4-1.** Obstacles to OBM implementation.

| Employees | Number of Companies Employees | | |
|---|---|---|---|
| | Total | Under 100 | Over 100 |
| Insufficient financial education for employees | 30 | 20 | 10 |
| Lack of follow-through | 19 | 12 | 7 |
| Bonus/reward systems not linked to financial results | 11 | 6 | 5 |
| Lack of leadership focus | 8 | 6 | 2 |
| Past initiatives that didn't work | 8 | 2 | 6 |
| Middle management resistance | 6 | 3 | 3 |
| Takes too much time | 6 | 3 | 3 |
| Incompatible with existing corporate culture | 4 | 1 | 3 |

when working with divisions or production facilities of large corporations that haven't adopted the open-book approach, but where the local leadership is committed to an open-book management approach, we have seen productivity and divisional profitability gains and measurable improvements in employees business knowledge.

With a good open-book management assessment a company can determine its own particular pitfalls and make a plan to deal with them. In this chapter, we'll call your attention to some of the more common pitfalls we've seen and suggest ways to avoid or minimize them.

## WHEN LEADERS LOSE FOCUS AND RESOLVE

Open-book practices challenge the heart and substance of leadership as the stories throughout this book reveal. Since open-book management is a way of running a business with a specific set of practices and

## ADVICE FROM THE FIELD

### "How to Avoid the Pitfalls"

The following bits of advice, most of them in one-liner, bite-size pieces, were lifted from the survey we conducted. The question from the survey generating these pithy gems and warnings simply asked respondents to provide some advice to other companies as they begin their journeys into deeper forms of open-book management:

You need a "champion" with credibility, sales skills, business knowledge, and the ability to manage "up" the organization.

Spend time getting people to understand that this is not as easy as it looks.

Have a two-year plan with all the steps to get you there.

Educate first, start slowly, do it completely.

Start with your vision and values first, then it will take hold.

Understand the cause-and-effect relationships that lead to the financial results.

To do open-book management, you must really want business partners.

Educate, educate, educate.

And one nay-sayer, and a few who ran into some trouble say:

Give open-book management a higher priority than we have.

Don't do it . . . share your results with those who can benefit from them.

Beware of the damage nonbelievers can do.

systems, the credibility of the leader's resolve is critical and must be demonstrated in what employees see the leader do. Jack Stack, CEO of Springfield Remanufacturing Corp., says leaders have to be willing to live in a glass house.

The closer to the action leaders can be for the first 12 to 18 months of implementation, the more rapidly the credibility and the trust will build. Correspondingly, the employee's commitment grows and use of the practice produces the business payback. Without a vision and a strong belief, leaders will become discouraged and revert back to their comfort zone. As a leader, you will need to do things differently to gain attention and convince others that you mean what you say. For example, increase your communication about the business and your accessibility. Clarity, commitment, and consistency are the watchwords.

## OVERCOMING THE "PLEASE-THE-BOSS" MENTALITY

The traditional structure for managing activities, tasks, and decision making in a company is through a command-and-control hierarchy. In most companies, an individual's performance review, compensation increases, bonus, and recommendation for advancement rest solely with the immediate supervisor. Is it any wonder that individual performers have focused on trying to please their bosses?

A dependency of very unhealthy proportions has developed in many companies. Open-book practices can do much to eradicate it, but while you are in the beginning stages of introducing OBM, please-the-boss thinking can be a big barrier to adoption. If an individual's thoughts and energy are being channeled to please another individual, when do they think and act for the business?

There are two solutions and both take a lot of work:

- First, open-book leaders must be diligent about redefining their roles. With team score cards tracking team results and the company financials, and with regular huddles, everyone becomes a business evaluator. Managers must realize they are *coaches*, shift out of the role of quarterly evaluator into that of helping others make it happen.
- Second, employees and managers alike can legitimately wonder whether those who are not pulling their weight will be truly accountable in an OBM system. In the companies that have been using the open-book approach for some years, like Foldcraft, the dynamic at play is peer-to-peer accountability, better known as *peer pressure*. This is much more effective than the boss riding herd on people to perform better. In open-book systems, accountability gets a lot of play and *results* are the primary feedback mechanism. We've heard managers say OBM makes it easier to eliminate the nonperformers because the basis for evaluation is factual and clear rather than subjective, and they can act more quickly. Over a specified time period, people either perform up to standards or they go away.

## DEALING WITH DOWNSIZING

Regardless of how responsibly an organization comes to the decision, letting people go is tough. Concern about people and the impact of joblessness on them is real and valid; concern about the financial performance and health of the company is also real and valid. OBM thinking allows you to address both with responsibility and integrity.

It can be especially tricky dealing with a significant downsizing that occurs in the early stages of, or because of, introducing OBM. In a division of one large corporation, when we were five months into the development of OBM, a reduction in force (RIF) was announced. It was the second such occurrence in 10 months. The previous RIF eliminated one-third of the employees from this division and some wounds were still very tender. Those that remained felt overworked; others clearly were running on empty.

The division president's motivation for adopting OBM had been, in part, a reaction to the employee response to the first RIF—many had asked, "Why didn't we have an opportunity to fix the problems and maybe save some jobs?" By contrast, in the downsizing that took place during the open-book introduction, there were few who were surprised. Rumors, as before, were plentiful. But this time the rumors were accompanied by discussion of the state of the business and the known factors that were putting pressure on the decision makers.

No, the RIF did not make people happy, but as one OBM team member said when she was tapped on the shoulder, "You know, its funny; I don't feel like a victim. I'm not taking it personally. I know it's a business decision." In fact, many saw the situation as somewhat more rosy than it would have been without OBM, "I'm more confident of my own business knowledge and I can now clearly articulate and sell my value to a potential employer."

## CONFRONTING US VERSUS THEM

Employees and managers are likely to misunderstand and misinterpret the open-book message in proportion to the current level of mistrust. We haven't been in a single workplace, including our own, where the potential for us versus them doesn't exist. If the chasm is deep, don't expect OBM to fix everything in six months or a year. But it will make us versus them more manageable.

While it is important in the management of any company to get people "on board," it is, in open-book management, paradoxically just as important to encourage different points of view and styles.

Us versus them is destructive to a business when it blocks communication, coordination, cooperation, and the teamwork needed to achieve the company's goals. With OBM, once the big picture is thoroughly understood, most people quite naturally move toward teamwork and, in fact, insist on it. Each wants some measure of control but all are tied to the same destiny.

In workplaces where there is intense Dilbert-like bitterness and numbness, the best route is to look for and work with *informal* leaders who are respected, not necessarily liked, by their coworkers. As these informal leaders shift their view and communicate by their actions, their change of heart will entice others—like a domino effect. Patience, encouragement, and education go a lot further in these climates than criticism.

A note of caution: In our experience, those leading the change can lose sight of their own connection to the very culture they are attempting to change. These champions, without guidance, can be right on the mark with their identification of problems, but unwittingly take steps and send messages that have the opposite effect than they intend. Outside coaching is very useful in the early stages of change.

## WHO'S IN CHARGE HERE?

We've heard many early OBM practitioners and interested managers wondering: Just how far does this "control thing" go? Recently, at one open-book company we know, employees became frustrated with their limited control over a couple of management decisions and policies. Two specific complaints were identified: first, they questioned why some business was accepted at a lower price and second, they complained about the expense of phone calls made by professional staff from airplane phones.

Once educated, empowered, and given a real stake in the outcome, employees can become forces to be reckoned with. This is a *good* thing. This is what you want. But you have to handle it properly. These questions and concerns, we advised, can and should be used for further education and deeper understanding of the company's short- and long-term goals and business strategy.

Employees needed to—and had a right to—understand why some business was accepted for a lower than normal price, and the business reasons behind the air phone expense. Managers need to capture these moments as opportunities rather than taking offense that their judgment was questioned. This is a good example of accountability. In open-book companies, accountability goes all ways and the explanations, that is, the accounts, of these activities provide the opportunity for business education in real time.

These kinds of situations also present good opportunities to clarify boundaries and to articulate the criteria used for decision making. Open-book practices do not guarantee that everyone in the company gets input on every decision, perhaps not even on the decisions that affect them directly. Rather, each position carries certain responsibilities that require a mix of decision making—by individuals, by teams, by groups outside the team.

Each employee needs to know which decisions they're held accountable for. But each person, as a member of a larger whole, also has a right to *inquire about and know* the business thinking behind decisions made by others, especially those that affect them. The process of learning what's behind decisions and policies is often enlightening. The questions can also cause the decision makers to rethink and make changes. The resulting learning helps the organization to keep evaluating and improving its results.

Related to decision making is the question of control. Hierarchy doesn't go away in open-book companies. Some people have more control than others. That said, it is important to reinforce continually the idea that everyone in an OBM company has significant control:

- Through business financial education, creating a line of sight, and understanding all the business interdependencies, employees learn what they do as well as what others do to influence outcomes.
- Their understanding stimulates a higher level of thinking so their ideas and problem solving shape the conclusions others make and the actions they take.
- Since control is often a matter of perception, once employees see the constraints imposed on companies by customers, competition, economic conditions, and available resources, they see that all control has limits and interdependencies.

When all is said and done, there's a simple rule of thumb that makes open-book companies successful: Focus on trying to control *the business* rather than individuals.

## STOP! I WANT TO GET OFF!

It is our experience that most companies are attempting to do more with less and many workers and managers have very full plates. Open-book implementation offers many choices, activities, and expectations. It is demanding and can be daunting. It takes some mighty steady leadership to focus the company and choose to do what can be done well.

In one company, our OBM design team was in the middle of a planning workshop when one team member began to note how much time was going to be required to "do it right." Looks of discouragement came across many faces in the room. "Yes, but . . ." questions began to pop up.

We asked the company president to make a judgment call. Could the people he was counting on to lead the OBM effort really get it done? He then reviewed with the team the components of the company vision and the challenges in the business plan and made sure to connect the work of each of the team members to the business goals. Then he challenged each person to examine the activities they were involved in and find one or two things they could let go of. He made it clear to all that he wanted OBM to succeed at his company. No waffling, no unrealistic "You can do it all" speeches, just plain, practical priority setting and business focus.

## GUARDING AGAINST A LACK OF FOLLOW-THROUGH

Here's some peoples idea of implementing OBM: Everyone in the company gets sheepdipped into a financial education class or a bonus is set up and, *voilà*, the company's now open book. Too extreme? We wish it were.

Open-book management is values and vision driven, and it won't work unless it gets into the nitty-gritty of your business. Our survey highlights just how many managers are attracted to the *philosophy* of open-book management, but the philosophy without a well-tuned set of practices is not enough. Sharing financials can set the right tone of trust and accountability, but then so much more needs to be done.

Our survey also shows that most companies have opted for variable pay tied to company results as a way to boost the learning in the company—a good move, mainly. The problem is that motivated ignorance is not much better than demotivated ignorance. Leaders need to use the bonus for education and motivational reasons and then use lots more.

Open-book management is not a program. It is a way of managing a business. It is a set of interlocking systems and practices that can't be implemented in a classroom. You have to get out on the field with good dedicated coaches and run the plays—over and over again. It is part of becoming professional business-smart players.

Manager follow-through is one of the most critical practices. If managers don't model the change it is highly unlikely that much change will be sustained. As in the many examples provided through the chapters in this book, repetition by leaders is a key ingredient for success.

## TOO MUCH TRAINING AND NOT ENOUGH LEARNING

Training and learning are two different things. While the classroom can support the learning process, the real-life events of the business, as discussed in staff and problem-solving meetings, are the real-time education. Much of the difficulty companies have with financial and other training is that they don't use other learning opportunities.

All too often we find well-meaning trainers or internal consultants who spend most of their time (and too much of everyone else's) instituting procedures, reviews, and training programs that have little or no strategic connection to the needs of the business. Their efforts seem to exist on a separate plane from the rest of the company and are often viewed by employees as superfluous or a nuisance. Open-book practices require most human resource professionals to reinvent their role. They have to have their own line-of-sight to corporate goals and be held accountable for outcomes. To do that they first need to learn about the business.

## WHERE YOU STAND DEPENDS ON WHERE YOU SIT

Positions in organizations are important; they embody goals, achievement, and status. Most people work their whole careers to reach a certain level or title. Unfortunately, they're usually climbing a ladder inside a silo—salespeople stay in Sales, accountants in Accounting, line workers on the line. This kind of career advancement creates myopia and a disproportionate concern for individual roles at the expense of the overall business.

Open-book practices tend to open everyone's perspective quite a bit, but the growing pains are unique for each role. Here's a look at some of the common OBM sticking points—and strengths—through each position's particular lens:

### CEO

*Strengths of the Position:*
- Has the final say.
- Sets the tone for the culture, vision, and more.
- Selects other members of the management team.

*Weaknesses of the Position:*
- Often isolated and removed from day-to-day operations.
- Often focused too much on external issues; internal focus suffers.
- Suffers from please-the-boss syndrome; often receives filtered, sugar-coated information.

*Advice:*
- Create a long-term open-book plan; avoid quick fixes.
- Communicate, communicate, communicate.
- Seize every opportunity to tell the story of the business; capture teachable moments with anecdotes; set the tone for managers.
- Focus on motivating; celebrate victories and achievements.
- Attend to all facets of No-Kidding Ownership; reward and recognize.
- Create the Huddle system from the top down; use it to constantly teach the business.
- Have fun so others can.

## Sales Manager

*Strengths of the Position:*
- Constant customer feedback and contact with the marketplace.
- Often the point person for product development.
- Critical importance of sales numbers; built-in line of sight.

*Weaknesses of the Position:*
- Historically doesn't understand business or operations.
- Can go into overdrive with sales activity.
- Often underestimate the time it takes to do the job.

- Tend to give and respond to emotional motivation rather than numbers motivation.

*Advice:*
- Learn the business, operations, and finance.
- Take the time to think strategically while you are producing.
- Become a team player; be willing to give up commission structure based on volume in favor of gross or net profits.
- Rotate yourself into other types of work at the company to broaden your perspective.

**Finance Manager**

*Strengths of the Position:*
- Finger on the financial pulse.
- Access to the CEO and the Board.
- Already fluent in a powerful, universal business dialect.

*Weaknesses of the Position:*
- Generally viewed as a controller; reactive, not a strategist.
- Generally adopts silo-type thinking.
- Removed from day-to-day operations.

*Advice:*
- Don't hoard or be condescending about numbers and financial advice.
- Be a teacher—you are *crucial* in that role—multiply yourself across the organization.
- Serve the line organization and learn the business drivers in sales and operations that create the numbers.

**Human Resources Manager**

*Strengths of the Position:*
- The advocate for the people side of the business.
- Controls the training budget.

- Leverage and input across company boundaries: everyone hires, promotes, and trains.

*Weaknesses of the Position:*
- Usually not viewed as a "hard business" thinker.
- Caretaker role, usually viewed as less important than the core business.
- Not considered knowledgeable about business and operations.

*Advice:*
- Learn the business, operations, and finance.
- Take the lead training and compensation design role in OBM that is naturally yours.
- Force colleagues to think through OBM systems and implications; don't succumb to let line managers delegate OBM implementation to you with accompanying time pressure to rush the process.

## Training Director

*Strengths of the Position:*
- Can act as Chief Learning Officer, a powerful post in today's business culture.
- Can influence up and across organization with learning events.
- Can multiply effectiveness through contract trainers and consultants.

*Weaknesses of the Position:*
- Often underbudgeted; historically poorly connected to finance department.
- Staff position that may not be aligned well with line managers.
- Too often uses training events as tools instead of real-time, on-the-job learning.

*Advice:*
- Advocate the competitive advantage of learning.
- Blend the wisdom of your internal managers and employees as trainers with the best of the outside experts.
- Set up just-in-time learning opportunities.

## Operations Manager

*Strengths of the Position:*
- Controls most of the staff, budget, and resources.
- Intimate knowledge of the workings of the business, including expense control.
- Responsible for the big results and the customers' satisfaction.

**Weaknesses of the Position:**
- No direct view of the marketplace.
- Often too powerful or insular; tend to ignore input from the rest of the company.
- Often more results-oriented than people-oriented.

**Advice:**
- Connect with the salespeople and meet the customers.
- Lead and develop the people while managing for results.
- Teach operations to the staff groups.
- Teach the whole of the business as you learn it yourself.

With OBM, your company may get immediate results. More likely it will take a while. Don't judge too quickly and don't look only for tangible results. Look at your teamwork, communication, learning rates, and growing sense of employee pride as lead indicators that business literacy is taking root. It will bear fruit soon enough.

*Section Two*

# Implementation and Results in the Field

# 5

## Critical Numbers Know-How

### Developing the Ability to Think in the Common Language of Business

*Open-book management is really maximizing the resources of the company toward its objective of making money. That starts with a belief that everyone can learn and understand the financials of the Company at some level. At Foldcraft, we have several members who are functionally illiterate. They can just barely read and write their own names. And yet these individuals can learn some of the most basic truths about their own unit's critical numbers with a little extra help and creativity. The challenge becomes how to make the education fun and exciting and meaningful within your own organizational culture, but the payoff is real. A critical piece to the open-book puzzle is the belief that people can and want to understand the direct connection between what they do and how that affects the Company's success.*

Steve Sheppard
CEO
Foldcraft Company

The chapters in Section Two will show the OBM principles and practices we have been discussing *in action*. They contain specific suggestions and ideas from real-life open-book companies on how to operationalize the principles and practices of OBM. The examples of exercises and actions, the tools cited, the rich diversity of voices from the field will provide the reader with helpful ideas and tools to try.

As you hear voices from the field, you will see that each company's application of the practices will look slightly different. Indeed, open-book management should be modified to fit each company's style, business needs, resource availability, and leadership acumen. But in all cases, you will discover that attentive, disciplined effort to use the practices drives the learning deep into the organization—and the results are impressive.

Business owners, managers, and workers who hear about open-book management for the first time are attracted to the notion that every employee learns to understand the company's financial goals and track its progress using its financial statements.

Finance is the language of business, spoken mostly in numbers, ratios, and percentages. There are as many dialects as there are industries, and as many subdialects as there are companies, each shaping the basics to fit their particular situation.

Financial language, organized into statements, is a measure of how value is created by the interaction of three components:

- The products or services.
- The processes used to produce the products and services.
- The people employed to operate the products and services.

Three basic statements tell the story: An Income Statement represents how the company performs; the Balance Sheet represents the company's worth; Cash Flow shows the sources and the uses of the company's cash, much like an individual's checkbook.

In addition, most companies identify and track key ratios that show the relationship between some of the numbers. These are selected based on which indicators best show the progress that the business is making.

Languages establish norms by which people communicate. It follows that employees will understand the norms by which their company operates when they learn the numbers and what they mean. Unfortunately, most employees are in financial darkness, and many don't know that they are missing anything important.

Ann Bradley, a trainer and internal consultant at Central and Southwest Services, Inc., (owner of five utilities and based in Dallas) found out how much she didn't know in January 1995 when one of her colleagues introduced her to the business board game called *Profit and Cash:*

"What's all this debt-to-equity talk? And minimum cash on hand? That's not how I like my personal finances to look. And that finance person who was explaining all those ratios—earnings per share, solvency ratios, and return on equity. Where did he come from? I thought they just took care of the money and let us do the work."

**VOICES**

See the survey results on page 70.

### ☑ SURVEY

The results of our survey, presented in the Appendix, underscore Ann's experience. Insufficient financial education was found to be, hands-down, the biggest barrier to open-book implementation. The bar charts in Figure 5–1 tell the story. Less that one-third of companies with fewer than 100 employees, and only about 10 percent of companies with more than 100 employees scored themselves as highly proficient at sharing and understanding critical business numbers.

#7. Plot your company's current practices of open-book management on these scales:

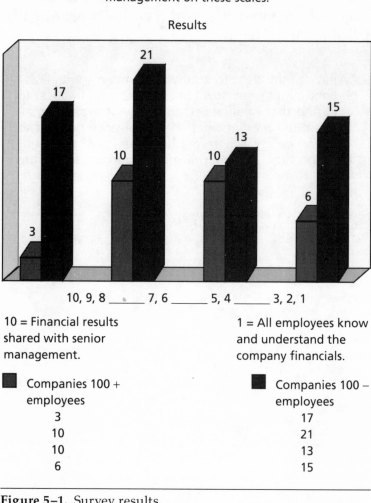

Results

10, 9, 8 _____ 7, 6 _____ 5, 4 _____ 3, 2, 1

| 10 = Financial results shared with senior management. | 1 = All employees know and understand the company financials. |
|---|---|
| ■ Companies 100 + employees | ■ Companies 100 – employees |
| 3 | 17 |
| 10 | 21 |
| 10 | 13 |
| 6 | 15 |

**Figure 5–1.** Survey results.

Jerome A. Harris, managing partner of American Express Tax and Business Services, Inc. formerly known as Checkers, Simon and Rosner in Chicago, is leading his firm toward the open-book approach within their own operation as well as by providing open-book services to the firm's clients:

> "The financial statements paint a picture of how your whole business is being operated. Each part of your statements will tell a part of the story. For example, let's say a business has quality problems and, for that reason, begins to have excessive sales returns. The income statement will put into financial terms what the present cost to the business is of those excess returns. It is important for your employees to benchmark the costs today and work on reducing the cost. In my experience, putting things into *dollars-and-cents* terms really brings home what the cost is to the business. For some reason, when businesses talk in percentages and other units of measure, the same impact is not there. People relate better to the information that some activity cost the company $1,000 in profit, rather than one unit in sales."

VOICES

## NETWORKING YOUR COMPANY'S INTELLECTUAL CAPITAL

In computer technology, individual PCs become more effective tools when they are networked so the users can make the right connections. PCs that have the software capability to access information combined with a user who knows the importance of the information and how to retrieve it provides more intelligence to the organization.

Similarly, if the different knowledge bases of each of your company's employees are linked to form a central, shared database, the business can make the most of its human brainpower. If the human knowledge carriers are then given a significant stake in the outcome, they are more satisfied and willing to reinvest their efforts into the success of the enterprise.

Computer technology has advanced to a point where different "languages" can talk to each other, which makes for increased capability and greater efficiencies. The same can be true when applied to networking the sales language with the operations language, with customer service language, with the R&D language, with the engineering language. The business financial language is the networking tool.

From Jerome A. Harris with an accountant's perspective:

**VOICES**

"Financial statements become the common denominator for bringing all aspects of your business together. You are no longer talking in engineering terms, sales terms, quality terms. You are discussing your business in one common term—dollars!

Businesses have increasingly become more complex and decisions have to be made faster. It has become virtually impossible for key executives to make decisions in the old command-and-control model. They need to push decision making down to lower levels, so it becomes imperative that all employees have access to financial information.

Empowering your employees to make critical decisions without the financial understanding of the impact of decisions is like driving a car blindfolded. It is a sure formula for disaster. I have a client who is a middle-market distributor of packaging products. He was pushing his salespeople to expand their sales base. In working with his salespeople, the CEO/owner focused on sales and related gross margins. He believed that would be enough information for his salespeople to model the type of customer they should be looking to capture. Well, without the salespeople understanding the whole financial picture, some unexpected things began to happen. Average inventory levels went up in greater relationship to sales because of new customer inventory requirements.

The same thing happened to accounts receivable in relation to sales. Interest costs skyrocketed and the company had a severe liquidity crunch. None of this company's salespeople had understood how the entire cost of attracting new customers worked. In helping this client work through the problem, we determined what had to be subtracted from gross profit to finally understand what profit was being made on each new customer. This was then tied to the financial statements.

Each month, the company's CEO and CFO meet with the salespeople who now know what a customer prospect should look like in financial terms, as well as, nonfinancial terms. Discussions of whether to take on new customers now center on long-term and short-term effects. If we don't continue to educate our workforce about the financial aspect of their decisions, we will surely not develop the type of empowered employee we need to assist us in building our business."

The rest of this chapter will introduce you, in some detail, to how some real-life companies have started to develop their ability to think in the language of business. The methods and exercises are as diverse as the companies themselves. The fun—and the payoff—will be in discovering what can work at your company.

## Getting Started at Amax West Coal

Amax West Coal, a division of Cyprus, is in the Powder River Basin, just north of Gillette, Wyoming. In its Eagle Butte mine, it has 12 house-sized trucks, with tires that cost $20,000 each. That gives you some idea of the maintenance costs. The trucks haul coal to the preparation plant where it is analyzed, crushed, and loaded by conveyor belt into 100-car trains headed to your local utility's power plant so you can toast your morning bagel and come home at night to a cool, centrally air-conditioned home.

**FIELD NOTES**

The economics of the coal industry have changed. Not too many years ago, companies could sell coal at $15 per ton in long-term contracts. Today, a growing spot market for short-term contracts has brought the price to as little as $3 per ton. Trucks and truck maintenance weren't that expensive in the era of good margins. They are very expensive in the era of shrinking margins.

One of Amax's team leaders in maintenance, Ken Benedict, took early steps to teach his team the financial side of their business. In an attempt to lower fixed overhead, maintenance crews had been kept lean and mean. During peak loads, work was contracted out.

Once, when one truck needed immediate maintenance, Benedict got the contractor's bid—$10,000—and decided to give his very busy crew a chance to beat it. His team noodled the problem, pulled out some spare and usable parts, figured out their own labor costs, and how they could fit the work in at one of their open bays. The price they quoted: $3,000 and change. Needless to say, they got the work. They also got the point: They could have a palpable impact on the bottom line.

When the case for business literacy was being considered by management, Benedict related this story as an example of how even basic financial know-how could have a powerful effect on employees and profits. The $7,000 in savings meant a lot, as did the pride of the maintenance crew. The possibility for more of the same convinced Amax to go open-book and teach its employees the financial statements, and the cost side of the business.

**FIELD NOTES**

## Paving the Way for OBM: A Not-for-Profit Breaks Down Its Bureaucratic Climate

OBM is as effective in a not-for-profit setting as elsewhere. Some of the techniques of business literacy don't apply. It is hard to peg a bonus, for example, to a certain profit level if there are no profits. But most organizations, for profit or not, have employees who need to know the big picture, have budgets, revenue streams and expenses, need to stay in the black, grow and use their resources efficiently, and hit certain performance measures.

In 1994, United Cerebral Palsy of King and Snohomish Counties (UCP/KS), a volunteer organization in Seattle with 350 employees, had just gone through its fifth executive director in ten years. As the fourth largest nonprofit agency of this nature in the country, UCP/KS was searching for some answers and new leadership to take it through a difficult transition.

Beginning as CEO in January 1995, Dr. Patrick Maynard immediately began meeting with board members and top management staff. Issues such as lack of trust, competition between key staff and programs, lack of accountability, declining initiatives, and an environment of smoldering hostility were commonly identified as the typical culture of the organization. Maynard thought OBM would provide many of the answers he was looking for, but first he had to wrestle with changing the highly unfavorable climate:

"UCP/KS was attempting to break out of its historical service philosophy of taking care of and protecting people with disabilities, to one of supporting people with disabilities in making choices and attaining as much independence as possible in their communities. This meant that UCP/KS had to change how they provided service, where they provided those services, and even when those services might be provided. A total transition of staff jobs, services, and even facilities was in order to make this transition happen.

**VOICES**

As I interviewed staff and met with individuals within the organization, I began to hear people talking about how ". . . all this change is too stressful." Although the board had made the service transition a priority, it lacked cohesiveness and commitment to the mission. The board was also very focused on process and micromanagement of the agency—contributing to the paranoid and defensive organizational culture. Eventually, after several board members resigned and were replaced the new board began to form a cohesive team that worked very hard to begin focusing on vision and policy."

Once the vision and mission were set, the challenge was to get communication processes in order. In Patrick Maynard's words:

"Communication was identified as: (1) creating an effective information dissemination process for a growing organization; and, (2) creating a culture of willingness and acceptance of open communication. The first one was quickly translated into reality with the creation of an Information Services Department (IS). The IS has been focusing on building the computer literacy of the staff, updating and building the network, and recently has begun to create an intranet for the purposes of internal training, support, and communication.

**VOICES**

The expected outcome of this staff training is the ability to push real-time information to line staff; giving them the ability, training, and support to make effective and timely decisions and to be accountable for those decisions. By pushing accountability and decision making down through the organization, there is no longer a need for supervisors. Their role becomes that of support, mentoring, resources, and training."

With the vision clear and the lines of communication open, the stage was set for financial literacy. Again, in Maynard's words:

**VOICES**

"The staff was receptive to learning finance, but the Finance Department had a difficult time releasing information, knowledge (and power), to the organization. Their ability to let go of their professional training to produce workable and understandable information was critical however, if UCP/KS continues to push decision making and accountability out to the furthest and lowest levels of the organization.

The acquisition of general knowledge of finance and resources has resulted in a staff who are more vested in the Agency through their grasp of the big picture. Where previously staff simply worked at their jobs with no concept of outcomes or relation to Agency mission—they are now thinking about what they do, at what costs, and how they might improve or change their jobs to more effectively transition themselves into the Agency's future."

**FIELD NOTES**

## Fear and Redemption at *Olathe Daily News*

Publisher Tim O'Donnell, like a lot of leaders we've met, began to practice OBM instinctively, before he knew there was a name for it. On May 11, 1996, which Tim now refers to as the day he started open-book management, he decided to level with employees about the troubling state of their company. Instead of seeing anger or discouragement on their faces, he was surprised to see relief and energy to meet the challenge. Here's Tim's account:

**VOICES**

"I had been at the company a year and was in the middle of a purchase contract that would allow me to manage the business and retain all profits. But it obligated me to pay the owners of the business nearly a quarter of a million dollars a year to do so until the sale was closed. Up to that point, I'd paid nearly $400,000 for the opportunity to lose about $250,000.

My employees thought I was crazy, the former owner/operator of the business was making money on a former albatross, my bank had to be questioning its initial belief that I was just the guy to turn around this business and my managers were scared and misdirected. Vendors were losing patience, customers were hearing rumors, and competitors were circling overhead.

I knew I had a long road ahead when I took over, but after one year, the honeymoon had ended. The company culture had reverted to the mistrust and suspicion I had initially found there. I remember sitting dumbfounded through an exit interview, as a sales rep described each decision I had made in hopes of effecting the turn around as another indication of our imminent doom.

That was it. I decided to assemble the entire company at the local Holiday Inn one Saturday morning. I started by telling the employees we were losing money and I told them how much. I shared some historical numbers about the business to give a frame of reference; in spite of losses, we were far ahead of the previous management. We were getting better. I told them about the purchase agreement with their former employers, and that time was ticking away. I told them we needed to immediately take measures to ensure bottom-line profitability. I told them I would understand if they felt it better to leave for more secure employment. I told stories, I elaborated on our vision, I asked for their energy to be renewed toward profit. I told them the truth. Not corporate-manager-truth. The whole truth.

During that meeting, something happened that will forever change the way I look at leadership and how I teach management. I found a way to harness an incredible force, almost like a force of nature. I stated that profit must always be part of our purpose and then, out of nowhere, I made a promise. I promised that each person would have access to our performance numbers at all times. I promised that the managers would begin in earnest to devise scoreboards or charts or some meaningful way to display performance. I told them I didn't exactly know how to do this, but that I would find a way if they were interested. Indeed they were.

By Monday the company had changed. People were asking questions, the word profit seemed to come up in every discussion. Our employees came alive. We managers, however, were stumped. We found it difficult in the ensuing weeks to adequately deliver on my promise to display our performance. Some of the first proposals were well meaning but not very good, and we knew it. We were trying very hard but had no real path or direction. Generally, we all agreed we needed to share more information with our people but couldn't agree on what to share or how to share it. Just posting numbers seemed hollow without sufficient understanding by all as to what reality these numbers exposed.

During my monthly visit to a local bookstore, I noticed a book titled *The Power of Open-Book Management.* Serendipity strikes. Finally some answers to our questions. As I was plodding along trying to frame our new approach, I was speaking to our company's benefits consultant and told her what was going on. She casually mentioned she had a friend who had written a book about something like what I was trying to describe. She arranged a lunch for me with her friend Jill Carpenter, author of the very same book I was engrossed in.

With Jill's help and lots of study, we have taken our company from a 9 percent loss to an average pretax profit for the current quarter of $15,000 a week, an incredible 18 percent. All in less than 6 months from the fateful meeting and less than 90 days after we started. The methods taught to us were direct answers to questions we had about running our company. The beauty of it is that there is no cookie cutter approach to implementation, each company participates in brewing their own special, homemade version of this business delicacy."

## "Playing Games" for Fun and Profit at ADVO

**FIELD NOTES**

No matter what their education, many people don't see themselves as capable of learning financial thinking. Maybe they don't understand the numbers and are embarrassed to say so, or perhaps they have acquired a learning block stemming from negative experience in school. As with any new learning activity, it's best to start with the basics and provide an opportunity for some enjoyment during the learning. The best approaches that we've seen involve creativity, personal interest, and interactivity.

At ADVO, Inc., a Connecticut-based billion-dollar-plus microtargetter of direct mail marketing, Gary Rosentreter and Frank Talz, head up the organizational development and training efforts. When operating at a 4 percent profit margin, it isn't easy to reinvest in tools, much less training and system development, but

Gary and Frank feel that business literacy and financial know-how are critical to ADVO's bottom line and a good complement to the company's self-directed work team structure. So they came up with a unique approach to getting the message across:

"Our approach to teaching business literacy is comprehensive. We use a video in which our chairman explains the basic elements of how ADVO makes money and defines some of the key leverage points—areas within our business where we can make critical decisions. The Organizational Development team has spent a full five days with each Regional SDWT (self-directed work team) training them on various subjects, including business strategy, cash management, and computer skills. A critical part has been the use of a *Making Money* simulation game that was developed specifically for ADVO. It uses real ADVO terms, markets, and situations."

**VOICES**

An interactive experience, such as ADVO's *Making Money,* is an excellent way to help employees learn and apply the learning in their own sphere of influence. We have seen enormous success using the business board game *Profit and Cash,* created by our company four years ago. The basic game creates various business scenarios and score is kept according to three performance measures: profitability, debt-to-equity, and cash on hand. As with most board games, the roll of the dice varies the outcome and keeps the game lively while opening up new learning.

Even without a simulation game, you can teach the basic concepts of business finance by relating them to something everyone has some experience with—their personal finances. Most employees manage household budgets, plan for the future, kids' educations, and retirement, for example, and make choices about how to allocate their dollar resources against current demands and perceived future needs. If they understand those dynamics, you can teach them the dynamics of your business.

**HANDS-ON
LESSONS**

## Thinking and Analyzing in Financial Language

The following exercise allows individuals to work from the base of knowledge they are intimately familiar with—their own finances. To start, provide an example of a personal Income Statement (see Figure 5–2) and Balance Sheet (see Figure 5–3). Then walk through it line by line asking questions to test understanding as you go. Facilitate and lead a conversation that encourages participants to discover both the positive and negative consequences of financial management:

1. Invite people to learn about how a particular decision can relate to both the long-term and short-term. For example, if a family takes on more debt, how does it affect its monthly expenses?
2. Highlight the impact of an unexpected event on an original plan. For example, what if the car needs major repairs?
3. Illustrate how the income statement and balance sheet are structured to help families stay on top of their finances.
4. Develop connections and insights between personal financial management and business financial management. An example: What is the financial reason that you would buy a house? How do these equate to business?

Ask about the types of decisions that can and must be made in a household context. Ask what-if questions that encourage thinking and discussion:

- What if the teenager in the family wants a new pair of $200 Nikes?
- What if this teen has seen the balance in the checkbook immediately after the deposit of the monthly paycheck?
- What if one of the parents is job searching, or has a need for new clothing?
- What if the family car gets sideswiped in the grocery store parking lot?
- What if the family decides it wants to buy a larger house in three years?

*(continued)*

*(Continued)*

Well-designed questions invite people to learn about how value can be added to decision making through understanding the larger context and knowing the goals of the enterprise. Good questions highlight the balance required between short- and long-term needs. This prepares them to go to the next step to learn more, and to apply it to a business situation. (See Figures 5–4 and 5–5.)

| Revenue | Year | Monthly |
|---|---|---|
| Earnings (personal income) | $20,000.00 | $1,666.67 |
| Interest income | 20.00 | 1.67 |
| | | |
| TOTAL REVENUE | $20,020.00 | $1,668.34 |
| | | |
| Expenses | | |
| Rent | $ 6,000.00 | $   500.00 |
| Day care | 3,600.00 | 300.00 |
| Food | 2,600.00 | 216.66 |
| Utilities | 1,200.00 | 100.00 |
| Insurance | 2,400.00 | 200.00 |
| Interest expense | 1,000.00 | 83.34 |
| Medical expense | 700.00 | 58.34 |
| Auto expense | 1,200.00 | 100.00 |
| Clothing | 300.00 | 25.00 |
| Entertainment and gifts | 600.00 | 50.00 |
| | | |
| TOTAL EXPENSES | $19,600.00 | $1,633.34 |
| | | |
| NET INCOME (What you have left over) | $   420.00 | $   35.00 |

**Figure 5–2.** Sample Income Statement.

*(continued)*

*(Continued)*

ASSETS (All the things you have)
  Current Assets (Can be converted to cash quickly)

| | |
|---|---:|
| Checking account | $ 100.00 |
| Savings account | 2,000.00 |
| Life insurance (Cash value) | 1,000.00 |
| Total Current Assets | $ 3,100.00 |

  Property (Items you can convert into cash if needed)

| | |
|---|---:|
| Automobile | $11,000.00 |
| Furniture | 3,000.00 |
| Tools and equipment | 1,000.00 |
| Total Property | $15,000.00 |

| | |
|---|---:|
| TOTAL ASSETS (Everything you have of value) | $18,100.00 |

LIABILITIES (What you owe others)
  Current Liabilities (must be paid for in near future)

| | |
|---|---:|
| Automobile loan | $ 7,500.00 |
| Credit card balances | 2,500.00 |
| Total Current Liabilities | $10,000.00 |

  Long-Term Liabilities

| | |
|---|---:|
| Loan from grandpa (due in 2110 A.D.) | $ 5,000.00 |
| Total Long-Term Liabilities | $ 5,000.00 |

| | |
|---|---:|
| TOTAL LIABILITIES (Everything you owe) | $15,000.00 |

EQUITY (The money you've managed to keep)

| | |
|---|---:|
| Net earnings (as of end year) | $ 420.00 |
| Retained earnings (Life's net earnings) | 2,680.00 |
| Total Equity (Net Worth) | 3,100.00 |

| | |
|---|---:|
| TOTAL LIABILITIES AND EQUITY | $18,100.00 |

**Figure 5–3.** Sample Balance Sheet.

*(continued)*

*(Continued)*

| Revenue | Year | Month |
|---|---|---|
| Earnings (personal income) | $ _____ | $ _____ |
| Interest income | _____ | _____ |
| _____ | _____ | _____ |
| _____ | _____ | _____ |
| _____ | _____ | _____ |
| _____ | _____ | _____ |
| _____ | _____ | _____ |
| _____ | _____ | _____ |
| _____ | _____ | _____ |
| _____ | _____ | _____ |
| **TOTAL REVENUE** | $ _____ | $ _____ |
| | | |
| Expenses | | |
| Rent | $ _____ | $ _____ |
| Day care | _____ | _____ |
| Food | _____ | _____ |
| Utilities | _____ | _____ |
| Insurance | _____ | _____ |
| Interest expense | _____ | _____ |
| Medical expenses | _____ | _____ |
| Auto expenses | _____ | _____ |
| Clothing | _____ | _____ |
| Entertainment and gifts | _____ | _____ |
| _____ | _____ | _____ |
| _____ | _____ | _____ |
| _____ | _____ | _____ |
| _____ | _____ | _____ |
| _____ | _____ | _____ |
| _____ | _____ | _____ |
| _____ | _____ | _____ |
| **TOTAL EXPENSES** | $ _____ | $ _____ |
| | | |
| NET INCOME (What you have left over) | $ _____ | $ _____ |

**Figure 5–4.** Your personal worksheet—Income Statement.

*(continued)*

**(Continued)**

ASSETS (All the things you have)
   Current Assets (Can be converted to cash quickly)
      Checking account            $ _____
      Savings account             _____
      Life insurance (Cash value)     _____
      Other                   _____
        Total Current Assets      $ _____

   Property (Items you can convert into cash if needed)
      Automobile               $ _____
      Furniture                _____
      Tools and equipment       _____
      Other                   _____
        Total Property          $ _____

TOTAL ASSETS (Everything you have of value)    $ _____

LIABILITIES (What you owe others)
   Current Liabilities (must be paid for in near future)
      Automobile loan           $ _____
      Credit card balances       _____
      Other                   _____
        Total Current Liabilities    $ _____

   Long-Term Liabilities
      Loan                    $ _____
      Other                   _____
        Total Long-Term Liabilities   $ _____

TOTAL LIABILITIES (Everything you owe)     $ _____

EQUITY (The money you've managed to keep)
   Net earnings (as of end year)     $ _____
   Retained earnings (Life's net earnings)   _____
      Total Equity (Net Worth)      $ _____

TOTAL LIABILITIES AND EQUITY        $ _____

**Figure 5–5.** Your personal worksheet—Balance Sheet.

# Seeing the Lights Go On in Tell City

As employees become increasingly comfortable and curious, they start asking questions about their company's expenses, profitability, accounts receivable, or retained earnings. Additional breakthroughs occur.

Sue Rye, the training manager at the bank in Tell City, Indiana, had open-book management on her mind. Sue had gone to an OBM seminar, and the concepts made sense. The more she read about OBM, the more the practices and principles seemed logical and smart. She read articles about OBM, and the concepts made more sense. So she decided to more ahead with financial education at the bank.

Using *Profit and Cash*®, Sue divided her employees into 14 teams to learn about their own and their customer's businesses. The results of the team play are shown in Figure 5–6. Sue tallied the results and posted them to heighten employee interest and to teach them about their own success and learning levels. An important outcome, and one Sue reinforced more aggressively as she saw her coworkers' lights going on, was how the teams would have reached more of their stated goals if they would have consistently kept them in mind.

As Sue put it, "As the players kept evaluating one move at a time, they would lose sight of the big goals. And they would miss opportunities to reach their goals." Thus the learning experience reflects the realities of what happens in companies that are *not* open-book—people get so focused on their immediate work that they forget how it connects to the overall success of the business. And they work hard at doing what can turn out to be the wrong thing.

BANK COMPARISONS
Relative to Greater Surpassing of Goals

Profitability 10%
Debt to Equity 1:1
Cash on Hand $20,000

| NAME | PROFIT | +/–GOAL | SOLVENCY | +/–GOAL | CASH | +/–GOAL | OVERALL | |
|---|---|---|---|---|---|---|---|---|
| | | | *Achieved or Surpassed All Three (3) Goals* | | | | | |
| The Bank | 44.6% | 4.46 | .95 | .05 | $45,000 | 2.25 | 2.25 | |
| Buzzard Roost | 32.3% | 3.23 | 1.00 | .00 | $49,000 | 2.45 | 2.23 | 29% |
| Bob's Bank | 38.6% | 3.86 | .68 | .32 | $27,000 | 1.35 | 1.84 | |
| Ice Bank | 34.3% | 3.43 | .81 | .19 | $23,000 | 1.15 | 1.59 | |
| | | | *Achieved or Surpassed Two (2) Goals* | | | | | |
| Big Bucks Bank | 49.5% | 4.95 | .74 | .26 | $16,000 | .80 | 2.16 | |
| Tell City Bank | 50.0% | 5.00 | .45 | .55 | $14,000 | .70 | 2.10 | |
| NUNYA | 18.8% | 1.88 | 1.10 | –.10 | $31,000 | 1.55 | 1.110 | 43% |
| 1st Butt Kickers | 19.7% | 1.97 | 0.00 | 1.0 | $ 7,000 | –.035 | 1.107 | |
| Holy Rollers | 16.0% | 1.60 | .84 | .16 | $13,000 | .65 | 0.80 | |
| Birthday Bank | 09.7% | 0.97 | .79 | .21 | $21,000 | 1.05 | 0.74 | |
| | | | *Achieved or Surpassed One Goal* | | | | | |
| FIBB | 24.0% | 2.4 | 1.21 | –.21 | $15,000 | 0.75 | 0.98 | 14% |
| First Nat'l | 03.3% | 0.33 | 1.0 | .00 | $ 5,000 | 0.25 | 0.19 | |
| | | | *Achieved or Surpassed Zero (0) Goals* | | | | | |
| Super Bank | 02.0% | 0.20 | 1.76 | –.76 | $ 2,000 | 0.10 | –0.15 | 14% |
| Hoosier Bank | –25.0% | –2.50 | 6.0 | –5.0 | $16,000 | 0.8 | –6.7 | |

**Figure 5–6.** Profit and cash results.

FIELD NOTES

## Customized Learning at Central and South West Services, Inc.

Building a bridge from general financial learning to your company's special brand of "financialese" can be accomplished in many ways. Customizing the teaching tools to reflect your specific business accelerates the learning process, propelling participants to higher levels of thinking and performance.

Ann Bradley, training consultant at Central and South West Services, Inc., a large utility company, accelerated her business acumen and the value she added to her business by spearheading the development of the customized business game for her organization. She focused on CSW's four performance keys—Profitability, Return on Equity, Earnings per Share, and Debt to Equity.

CSW now teaches a two-day class called Open-Book Leadership (OBL) that includes their business game. Each CSW manager works through specific ways to use the open-book training and ties it to goals already in place. Using Capital Connections' four-dimensional model (the principles illustrated in Chapters 4 to 7 of this book), participants create action plans (Figure 5–7).

Ann and her team designed an action-packed workshop that helped participants apply their financial learning to their everyday issues and concerns. One reason it was so effective is that they did their homework. In addition to outside resources, they used people in their own organization who speak the language of operations, finance, management development, and engineering. These are the people who can guide and reinforce the application to the daily activities and thereby gain results more quickly.

The effectiveness of the training class is measured by business results. The memo shown in Figure 5–8 is an example of their Open-Book Leadership success.

**Player-Coach Leadership**

| *Practices* | *Actions* | *By When* | *Resources* | *Milestones* |
|---|---|---|---|---|
| Creating community where everyone feels a part of the team and has a shared purpose. | Solicit input through group team meetings. Spread information about business standings. | ASAP December 1996 | None outside Income Statement | Know fundamentals of Business. Share critical numbers. (downtime, start-up time outage, overhaul costs; impact on bottom line) |

**Critical Numbers Know-How**

| *Practices* | *Actions* | *By When* | *Resources* | *Milestones* |
|---|---|---|---|---|
| Educating every employee on the "big picture" and the part they play in it. | Develop scorecard. Review situations and explain how they affect you. (Business Quarterly Report) | ASAP June 1997 | Work teams Operations department | Use to tract performance Share critical numbers Focus on targets (Bus Bar Costs) |

**No-Kidding Ownership**

| *Practices* | *Actions* | *By When* | *Resources* | *Milestones* |
|---|---|---|---|---|
| Informal recognition is frequently given for work well done, and victories are celebrated. | Recognition during meetings. | Monthly department meetings. | Employees Fellow supervisors | Stories that recognize individuals are told. Leaders are developed. |

**Intensive Huddle System**

| *Practices* | *Actions* | *By When* | *Resources* | *Milestones* |
|---|---|---|---|---|
| Recognizing that communication is a leader's top priority responsibility. | Provide proper information behind numbers. | ASAP | Regional Coach/ Supervisor | Weekly "tailgates" focused on plant performance. |

**Figure 5–7.** Mr. West action plan.

Memo

From:      Jim Peck
Dept:      CENTRAL MAINTENANCE FACILITY
Subject:   Open-Book Stories

Thought ya'll would want to share in this success story. John just attended the session this week. Hey, this OBL stuff really works!

Jim

"Seest thou a man diligent in his business? He shall stand before kings; he shall not stand before mean men."

Proverbs 22:29

**Forwarding note from SCIS457—VMPROFS 08/22/96 15:59**

To:        STSO196—VMPROFS Jim Peck
From:      Welsh x637
Subject:   Open-Book Stories

Here's an OBL story . . . I got back to the plant and checked on the $500,000 inventory reduction work that was in progress since July 1st and due to be finished by Aug. 31st. We were at $290,000 with a week to go; I thought this is a good place to start, so we met at the start of work this morning where I had a chance to ask questions, Does anyone know we are trying to reduce inventory? (several did); if anyone knew how many dollars in inventory we have (only one knew); then I was able to explain how much inventory we had, what it costs us to carry inventory per year (and per month), how much longer we had to get the $500,000 out of inventory and where we were. I challenged them to help find some parts that we will never use that we can write off while we have this opportunity, and offered to get enough pizza out here to feed everyone if we get the full amount out by Aug. 31st. (One of the employees owns a pizza cafe so we will get the pizza from him.)

Several of the crafts people have jumped ion to help the stores people, where prior to this we couldn't get much response. There is no doubt in my mind now we are going to the $500,000 prior to Aug. 31st. I'm going to use this to post results every day on a thermometer chart and a timeline graph and help get the OBL ball rolling here.

Just a story that you taught us about.

John

---

**Figure 5–8.** Jim Peck memo.

## Teaching the Language of Your Business

**HANDS-ON LESSONS**

Your goal should be to have each specialist at your company—sales, production, distribution, customer service—be able to translate their specialty into your company's financial language.

A good exercise is to go line item by line item through your company or division income statement, or budget, providing an explanation and clarification for each term and what goes into it. A simplified example of a chart that you can use follows. Tell stories including real events and people to illustrate how people impact, influence, and are part of what goes into making up the numbers. For example:

- **Revenue:** Our company is planning to grow. We are planning on serving 30 percent more customers in the next two years. As we invest in more resources to sell and service, it is critical to our success to bring in the revenue dollars in the timeframe needed to help pay for the added expenses. On the business plan, the 10 percent growth for this year shows up primarily in our projections for our two busiest quarters. Here's our pro forma income statement.

- **Expenses:** We've got to be careful not to increase our spending too fast. This would put us in danger of running out of cash, and yet we need to be sure we have the additional people and material to meet the demand created by bringing in new customers. We need to track our spending carefully and make new judgment calls as we grow. The increase in administration, salary, and sales expenses is planned each quarter to match the portion of expected growth in revenues.

- **Profit Margin:** After studying the industry, our competitors, and our company's capability to remain healthy and to grow our business along with our investor obligations, we determined that we need 15 cents out of every revenue dollar as profit this year (15% profit margin) and 18 cents next year (18% profit margin).

*(continued)*

*(Continued)*

If we meet the revenue targets for the second and third quarters and we manage our expenses within the numbers we talked about for administration, salaries, and increased sales expenses, we will be on goal for this year. We do have some concern that ABC supplier might increase their prices, which could jeopardize our ability to reach the 15 percent goal. Joe is meeting with Sarah Smith at ABC next week to get the facts on this.

• **Return on Equity:** In order to purchase 25 PCs and the needed software to track delivery to new customers in the new service area, we're financing the purchase through an investment from MM group. This adds $_____ to their original investment. By the end of the second year of our growth, MM group expects to be earning 12 percent on their investment.

Each opportunity to review this type of business information gives employees another practice round and the chance to sharpen their business thinking. Chapter 8 on player-coach leadership points to how crucial this role of teaching, communicating, and coaching is for leaders in an open-book culture.

**FIELD NOTES**

## Continual Business Learning at Foldcraft

At Foldcraft, where they make restaurant and other institutional furniture, creativity and fun permeate their financial education. And they are especially wise—they send the message, like Tim O'Donnell at *Olathe Daily News,* about how important the learning is by having their CEO, president, and CFO involved in leading their creative learning events.

This is how Steve Sheppard, CEO, describes Foldcraft's financial education:

"Creating is the operative word when it comes to educating. The financial education process at Foldcraft began with a voluntary lunchtime program wherein the company's president, Chuck Mayhew, compared the typical finances at home with the finances of the business, in as simple a fashion as possible. At one point, he compared the process of baking chocolate chip cookies with the building and costing of a product, and actually baked the cookies to drive home his point!

**VOICES**

The success of this simple approach prompted us to a second generation of teaching and to mandate these sessions for the balance of the organization. The third generation saw the creation of the School Desk Company game, which referenced one of our foreign operations in allowing participants to apply the concepts learned during earlier sessions. The fourth generation of financial education is being developed at present and will focus on a better understanding of the balance sheet. But the important realization for us is that we need to continue planning for ongoing open-book education and do it with new approaches. There is real excitement in seeing employees' joy and elevated self-esteem in making fundamental financial connections. Sometimes it leads us to silently pump fists and mutter "Yes!" under our breath. The process is exhilarating."

## The Importance of Scorecarding at Web Converting

We all tend to respond to what is in front of us, to what is most urgent. And we get sidetracked easily. Even if we know the overall business numbers well, we can get derailed, more readily than we like to admit, by the immediate issues and emergencies in any work day. The real challenge in developing the Critical Numbers Know-How is to be sure employee understanding dovetails with daily actions.

**FIELD NOTES**

At many OBM companies, individuals and teams track their progress, while keeping their eye on the goal, by using a scorecard. The story of what goes into making up the numbers becomes a story they are living—the people in marketing, in customer service, in accounting, in engineering can literally *see* their affect on the profitability of their company. Putting actual performance measures on a visible public board provides the team with a point of reference and constant reminder of the primary purpose of their work.

**HANDS-ON
LESSONS**

## Set a Target Number and Educate Employees on How to Improve It

1. Take a number from the income statement that needs to improve, whatever the industry or your company's unique cost structure deems critical. It could be payroll accuracy for a temp firm, or gross margin for a healthcare consulting firm or temporary labor expense for a contract assembly company (Figure 5–9). Another source for these numbers is to use the balance sheet where inventory and debt and other critical numbers appear. In most instances, the income statement is the easier place to begin and understand for nonfinancially trained employees.

2. Educate your team on what goes into making up the number.

3. Generate ideas on what will make the number go in the right direction.

4. Measure the number rigorously and regularly.

5. If the number goes in the right (or wrong) direction, analyze why.

| Revenue | 400 |
|---|---|
| Costs of Goods | 235 |
| **Expenses** | |
| • engineering | 8 |
| • insurance | 7 |
| • temporary labor | 18 |
| • travel | 12 |
| • advertising | 24 |
| • rent | 39 |
| • office | 27 |
| **Net Profit/Loss** | 30 |

**Figure 5–9.** Income Statement for Acme Products.

Scorecarding gives Rob Zicaro and his team at Web Converting a way to follow the action and keep score:

**VOICES**

"Reviewing monthly income statements is important but it only provided a history of what happened. We learned quickly that numbers representing our financial performance must be measured daily by each machine crew as the work is in progress. The number we use to measure our direct financial performance at each machine is called revenue per man-hour. This dollar amount per hour, for each person at a machine, is the most direct line of sight for each member of a work team. At any hour of the day, a machine operator and his or her assistant know whether a job is running at a profit. We know from our cost structure and overhead expenses our revenue per man-hour must be $50. If a job is not running at a profit, the quality tools of process improvement are applied to redesign the work and remove any unnecessary steps from the process. These improvements to work design illustrate how performance enhancements and financial success are interconnected."

A sample scorecard Rob and his coworkers use is shown in Figure 5–10. Through the scorecarding Rob describes further what he calls "making the line-of-sight real."

WO Production Report  Date:_____  Scheduled Hrs.: Start_____  Finish_____

MACHINE #:_____  Operator:_____  Shift:_____  Co-Workers:_____

| | | | Machine Hrs. | | | Personnel | Income Produced | | | Value Grossed Divided by |
|---|---|---|---|---|---|---|---|---|---|---|
| Job# | W.O.# | Customer | Set Up | Run Time | Down Time | Total Labor Hrs. | Prod. Out | Unit Price | Value Grossed | Total Labor Hrs. |
| | | | | | | | | | | |

Quality assurance check up: Start ☐ Middle ☐ End of shift ☐  Rework produced? Yes ☐ No ☐ Estimated time to fix:    Initial:

| | | | Machine Hrs. | | | Personnel | Income Produced | | | Value Grossed Divided by |
|---|---|---|---|---|---|---|---|---|---|---|
| Job# | W.O.# | Customer | Set Up | Run Time | Down Time | Total Labor Hrs. | Prod. Out | Unit Price | Value Grossed | Total Labor Hrs. |
| | | | | | | | | | | |

Quality assurance check up: Start ☐ Middle ☐ End of shift ☐  Rework produced? Yes ☐ No ☐ Estimated time to fix:    Initial:

| | | | Machine Hrs. | | | Personnel | Income Produced | | | Value Grossed Divided by |
|---|---|---|---|---|---|---|---|---|---|---|
| Job# | W.O.# | Customer | Set Up | Run Time | Down Time | Total Labor Hrs. | Prod. Out | Unit Price | Value Grossed | Total Labor Hrs. |
| | | | | | | | | | | |

Quality assurance check up: Start ☐ Middle ☐ End of shift ☐  Rework produced? Yes ☐ No ☐ Estimated time to fix:    Initial:

**Figure 5–10.** Production report.

**VOICES**

"The connection between financial success and performance is strengthened when production reports are filled out at the end of each shift and the machine crews calculate their revenue per hour. When team members leave for the day they know their revenue per hour and whether their job ran at a profit. This powerful line-of-sight is experienced at the end of every shift in our plant. Before measuring revenue per man-hour a person never knew if he or she made an impact on the profitability of the business. Now the picture is clearer and the goal is tangible. Once the production reports are completed they are entered into our information systems and the numbers are added into each team's road map."

A sample of the Film Team's *Monthly Road Map* is shown in Figure 5–11.

| Aug. 96 | | | |
|---|---|---|---|
| Breakeven | $194,500 | Prod. Report Value to Date | $128,049 |
| Proj. Sales | $300,016 | As % of Breakeven | 66% |
| Proj. Profit | $105,516 | As % of Proj. Sales | 43% |
| | | Work Days in Month | 22 |
| | | This Is Day # | 9 |
| | | Percent of Days | 41% |
| # of Unreported Prod. Reports | | MTD Rev/Man Hr. | $73.54 |
| | | | |
| | | MTD Jobs Shipped | 21 |
| Major Jobs and Proj. for Month: | | MTD Jobs on Time | 18 |
| | | MTD on Time % | 85.71% |

| Customer | Projected Machine Hrs. | Actual Machine Hrs. | Projected Revenue | Actual Revenue |
|---|---|---|---|---|
| ABC Corp. | | | $70,000 | $67,000 |
| TOP-ACCT. | | | $73,016 | $73,000 |
| Mass Port | | | $80,000 | $72,111 |
| Wilson | | | $25,000 | $14,994 |
| Jordan Marsh | | | $37,000 | $32,323 |
| Par-Moore | | | $60,000 | $52,001 |
| All Others | | | $25,000 | $22,500 |
| Total: All Custmrs | | | $300,016 | $334,833 |

**Figure 5–11.** Monthly road map.

## Scorecards Serve the Customer Focus at Schrock Cabinet Company

At Schrock Cabinet Company, each of the operating units ties its scorecard to a financial, to safety, customer satisfaction, and major corporate goals. And each has a clearly defined stake in the outcome. The program is called the Schrock "Success Sharing Plan." In the company newsletter, Merv Plank, Schrock's president, set the target measures for the operating units and explained their business value:

**FIELD NOTES**

"We chose Inventory Record Accuracy as our quality goal in 1996 because our ability to maintain accurate records of our inventory is critical to our ability to serve our customers with the right amount of product at the right time. On-time and complete delivery is essential to keeping our current customers happy and developing new business. Safety results not only impact our worker's compensation costs, but also are an indication of the quality of work life within the organization. By focusing on a safe work environment, we can provide a workplace that associates can be proud of."

**VOICES**

---

## Creating Your Own Line-of-Sight Map

To develop a line-of-sight map from your team to the company income statement, see Figure 5–12 for an example. Notice some of the unique terms. Then take a look at how the line-of-sight illustration (Figure 5–13) shows how an individual's activity can be traced to his or her impact on an income statement. Then create team scorecards to track your team's performance. Use the following criteria as a guide:

- Identify your team's outputs that contribute to your company's financial goals.
- Chart factors that vary with business activities or individual and team performance.
- Where appropriate, list individual contributors.
- Select factors to track that directly or indirectly have an impact on the financial performance of your company (this may require a discovery process, especially if your team is in a support role).

*(continued)*

**HANDS-ON LESSONS**

*(Continued)*

Support teams often scorecard their internal customers
expectations and needs. Human Resources might track
recruitment and hiring costs, expenses associated with
new hire training, or the expenses related to how long
it takes for new employees to be productive.

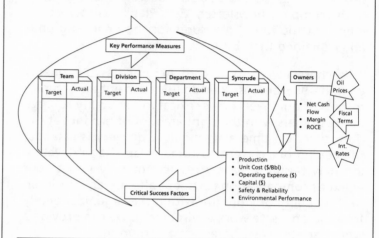

**Figure 5–12.**  A Canadian success story.

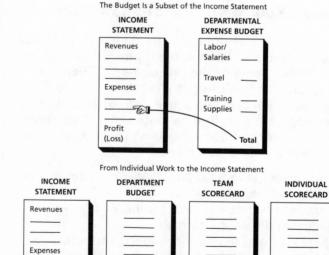

**Figure 5–13.**  Line-of-sight graphic.

Mark Stewart, director of human resources, explains how the program was introduced:

"Training on business fundamentals was being rolled out so associates could understand how they can impact the business and their success-sharing payout. Then large site boards were placed in each location to track the result. This helps focus the entire SCC team on its customers' needs and expectations."

**VOICES**

A sample of *Schrock's Operating Unit Goals* is shown in Figure 5–14.

---

Quality: Achieve Inventory Record Accuracy of 96% from 7/1/97–12/31/96

Delivery: Achieve order completion rate of 98% from 7/1/96–12/31/96

Safety: Achieve 5% improvement in lost time Incident Case Rate over a base period of full year—1995—results

SCHROCK CABINET COMPANY
SUCCESS SHARING PLAN

ARTHUR FACILITY

| Key Measures | Jul | Aug | Sep | Oct | Nov | Dec | Avg |
|---|---|---|---|---|---|---|---|
| Quality 96 | | | | | | | |
| Delivery 98 | | | | | | | |
| Safety 4.1 | | | | | | | |

---

**Figure 5–14.** Schrock's operating unit goals.

**FIELD NOTES**

## Developing a Corporate Scorecard at Syncrude

The development of a corporate scorecard puts key companywide outcomes in the limelight. It stimulates important discussions, strategic thinking, and creativity among the senior leaders of an organization. The spotlight does put some heat on management and requires an accounting to the entire organization for the big picture performance of the company.

In Figure 5–15 provided by Syncrude, each dial shows negative numbers on the left of the dial in red and positive numbers in green on the right of the dial. Using the same diagram, they show three different sets of numbers each month: Current Month, Year to Date, and Total Year Forecast.

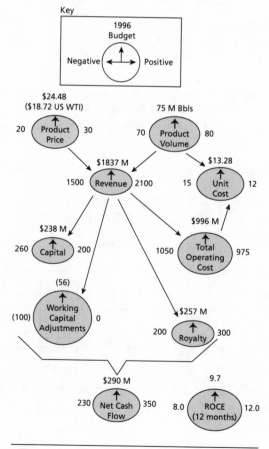

**Figure 5–15.** Corporate dashboard.

Figure 5–16 is an educational tool Syncrude uses to teach employees the meaning of the terms on the corporate scorecard. Don de Guerre, Syncrude's organization effectiveness leader, has guided change efforts at his company since 1989. The company had already established new vision and values, a set of Principles for Organizing Work (POW) and semi-autonomous work teams (SAWTs). Don describes the value of business literacy and scorecards:

"Business literacy was introduced to the company as a new paradigm—a new set of principles describing a new commonsense in which every employee thinks and acts like an owner of the business. It was developed to add to the existing set of principles. As part of its umbrella policy framework, Syncrude also has a set of principles to guide employee actions in other areas,

**VOICES**

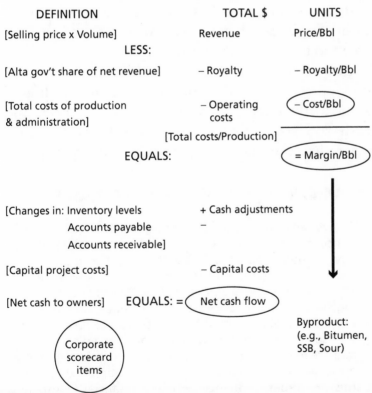

**Figure 5–16.** Corporate scorecard terms defined.

such as living the vision and the values, loss management, reliability, information systems, and environmental diligence. In the original POW, SAWTs were described as work teams that not only do the work, but also record or measure the work, analyze and problem solve the results, and then plan to continuously improve. The development of critical numbers know-how and the use of balanced scorecards provided a new means to make this principle real on the shop floor."

Many companies build their corporate scorecard by identifying their critical success factors. If, for example, customer satisfaction is a key indicator of competitive strength, then the financial measurement of customer satisfaction is defined—what losing one customer costs or the lifetime revenues of a customer. Everyone in the company then needs to understand how their decisions and actions influence these measures. Scorecards with lines of sight can then be used to keep teams accountable and focused on the business.

Other companies start with their business plan and develop companywide scorecards that have a line of sight to their income statement, balance sheet, and cash flow statement. Others create charts that track key ratios. The rule of thumb is: *Do what works!*

**FIELD NOTES**

## A Higher Level of Thinking at Foldcraft

As with any other language, being fluent in business finance means more than being able to translate literally. It means being able to *think* and *intuit* in the specific business finance dialect your company speaks. The nuances understood only after "living and breathing specific numbers" are the clues that guide an employee to seek out additional data, to act on a hunch that something's not quite right, to change direction in midstream because the current flow of activity isn't achieving its intended result. Once employees reach this broad-based fluency with the financial language of the company, they rise to the next level: *participative planning.*

At most companies, the planning process is broken into categories, such as Sales Projections, Marketing Plan, Capital Investment, Personnel Plans, Administrative Costs, Purchasing. Individuals or groups usually work on their own portion of the plan, but relatively few work on the *integration* of all the elements. A tremendous amount of intelligence is built up during the planning process but it stays, in most companies, in the heads of a few.

At command-and-control companies, the strategic business planners and senior managers know the value of starting with a well thought through plan and a keen awareness of the underlying assumptions that the plan sits on. As the year rolls on, they look at indicators that influence their assumptions and then make adjustments as things change. As managers alter their plans and decisions, they understand the underlying reasons, but often many of those carrying out these new decisions don't have a clue. And as a result they execute poorly, doing their jobs by rote, automatons instead of intelligent agents.

Imagine a company where everyone contributes to the plan, knows their role in it, the assumptions that underlie it, and the factors that can affect it (see Figure 5–17).

The leaders at Foldcraft imagined just that and set about making it happen. Steve Sheppard, CEO, talks about it this way:

"The most recent example of numbers-driven change at Foldcraft is in our sales planning process. In providing for a "planned, controlled growth," as directed in the company's Mission Statement, we know the level of growth that is both safe and healthy for the company. On that basis, sales and marketing personnel are charged with developing the specific plans that detail where that growth will come from and why, when we will expect to see the additional business during the year, and what contingency plans we will use to realize our growth rate in the event that sales of established products in anticipated markets do not materialize. The creation of plans such as these requires a comprehensive knowledge of the marketplace, to be sure, but also requires the sales and marketing personnel to understand the effects of their plans on the rest of the organization, and the ability of those people to control their own critical

**VOICES**

| Line Item | Line Item Owner(s) by Team Leaders | Plan | Current Actual | 30-Day Projection |
|---|---|---|---|---|
| **Sales** | Margo | 300,000 | | |
| Products | Sam, Tom, George | 100,000 | 120,000 | 90,000 |
| Services | Pam, Tom, Sarah | 200,000 | 198,000 | 210,000 |
| Discounts | Carla | <30,000> | <35,000> | <30,000> |
| **Net revenue** | Margo | 270,000 | 283,000 | 270,000 |
| | | | | |
| **Cost of sales** | | | | |
| Materials | Sue, Gail, Ken, Kim | 60,000 | 61,000 | 58,000 |
| Dir labor hrs. | Tom, Jim, Pat, Cyndi | 140,000 | 152,000 | 145,000 |
| | | | | |
| **Total cost of sales** | Ken | 200,000 | 213,000 | 203,000 |
| | | | | |
| **Gross margin** | Ken | 33.3% | 23.3% | 32.3% |
| | | | | |
| **G&A** | | | | |
| Salary | John | 30,000 | 8,000 | 8,000 |
| Rent | Carl | 5,000 | 5,000 | 5,000 |
| Office supplies | Laura | 200 | 150 | 250 |
| L.D. phone | Kathy | 800 | 820 | 790 |
| | | | | |
| **Total expenses** | | 36,000 | 33,970 | 34,040 |
| | | | | |
| **Net profit/loss** | | 34,000 | 36,090 | 32,960 |
| | | | | |
| **Net margin** | | 4.3% | 11.3% | 10.9% |

**Figure 5–17.** Income Statement.

numbers. Sales plans are no longer simply handed down from marketing management. Rather, they are becoming companywide consensus plans based on the need to control the critical numbers throughout the organization. Members of the entire company are responsible for achieving the numbers that allow the sales plans and contingency plans to be achieved."

As companies deepen their practices in the critical numbers know-how arena, they become increasingly aware of the endless opportunities for learning. The more employees learn, the more they discover that the learning never really ends—in part due to the normal changes in the business driven by changes in the economy, the industry and customer needs—and, in part due to internal changes such as the way different individuals respond to events, the consequences of past decisions, process improvements, new people in positions who come at issues and decisions differently. It goes on and on.

# 6

## The Intensive Huddle System

### Utilizing Your Organization's Intelligence

*Given the fast pace of business, it becomes very difficult to keep your organization focused. An excellent method for keeping focused is to cull from your financial statements those critical numbers to be benchmarked. But you will find, as a leader, that it will take considerable repetition on your part to insure that your employees: (1) understand what the critical numbers of the business really are; (2) understand that they must* own *the numbers; and (3) understand that they have the power to change* the numbers by their actions.

Jerome A. Harris
Managing Partner
American Express Tax & Business Services,
formerly known as Checkers, Simon and Rosner LLP.

**M**any careers have been built on an ability to access and manage information. It can be a great source of control and, traditionally, those who have it are cautious about sharing it, doling it out on a need-to-know basis. Open-book management requires a very different approach. Managing hierarchies of information that create connections and purpose is the key to creating business literacy as a strategic advantage.

When considering how information should flow in an open-book environment, biological systems, not mechanical ones, are the appropriate metaphors. Think of what runners have to do to make their bodies finish a race. The body manages information and biochemical activity on many levels at once—cells, cell clusters, muscles, nervous system, cardiovascular system all working simultaneously and in complete harmony. Similarly, the task for open-information companies is integrating the individual with the team, with the department, and with the company. And the goal is to integrate these levels both unconsciously—as with the runner's breathing—and consciously, as with the runner's decision to take a drink at the next water stop.

An OBM company must institute regular sessions or mechanisms of information exchange where the focus is on organic interaction: learning, adjusting, and reflecting on organizational effectiveness. We call this the *Intensive Huddle System.*

For the Huddle System to work, OBM leaders must, as suggested by Jerome A. Harris' quote at the beginning of this chapter, take on the constant role of communicator, teacher, and coach. The Huddle System is the open-book management professional practice field—the place where the business "players" develop a high level of performance and competence. As a communication system, it functions to focus the business on connecting the right data and information in real time, making sense of it as it relates to the company objectives, and making necessary adjustments to stay on track. The Huddles are an opportunity for employees to turn learning into intelligent application. If the Huddle System works, better quicker decisions are made and executed throughout the enterprise.

# A CLOSED LOOP OF INFORMATION AND ACCOUNTABILITY

While the practice of scorecarding, described in Chapter 5, keeps contributors focused in the midst of daily work action, in the Huddles, employees and managers have a chance to step back, reflect, analyze, refocus, and determine course corrections (Figure 6–1).

As you can see in Figure 6–1, the Huddle System functions as a closed loop of information and

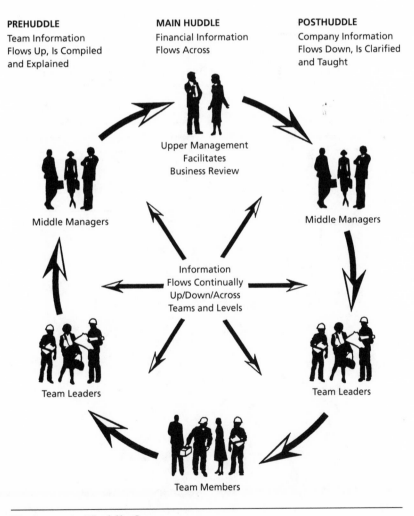

**PREHUDDLE**
Team Information Flows Up, Is Compiled and Explained

**MAIN HUDDLE**
Financial Information Flows Across

**POSTHUDDLE**
Company Information Flows Down, Is Clarified and Taught

Upper Management Facilitates Business Review

Middle Managers

Middle Managers

Information Flows Continually Up/Down/Across Teams and Levels

Team Leaders

Team Leaders

Team Members

**Figure 6–1.** Huddle System.

Team Scorecard (Performance Drivers)

| Order Processing Scorecard (A) | Administrative Scorecard (C) | Proposal Management Scorecard | Customer Satisfaction Scorecard |
|---|---|---|---|
| # Orders Activated:<br>   Current Month ____<br>   YTD ____<br><br># Disconnects:<br>   Current Month ____<br>   YTD ____<br><br>% Orders Entered<br>   Within 3 Days ____ | Headcount ____<br><br>Average YTD<br>   Employee<br>   Training Hrs. ____<br><br>Capital Expend. ____<br><br>Revenue per Head ____<br><br>Expense per Head ____ | **Proposals** / **Contract Modifications**<br>Submitted____ / Submitted____<br><br>Wins: (A) / Approved ____<br>   Month ____<br>   YTD ____<br><br>Losses:<br>   Month ____<br>   YTD ____ | Billing Disputes:<br>   Current Month ____ (B)<br>   YTD ____<br><br>Restoration<br>   Intervals ____<br><br>Number of<br>   Disruptions ____<br><br>% Customer<br>   Want Dates Met ____ |
| Team Members: Randy<br>           Dave<br>           Sharon | Team Members: Jack<br>           Richard<br>           Robin | Team Members: Scott  Steve<br>           Jane   Debra<br>           Susan  Ann<br>           Karen | Team Members: Chris<br>           Kim<br>           Alan<br>           Dan |

Division Scorecard (Division Financial Indicators)

| | Actual | Budget | Variance | Next Month Forecast | End of Year Forecast | Variance |
|---|---|---|---|---|---|---|
| Net Revenue | (A),(B) | ____ | ____ | ____ | ____ | ____ |
| Cost of Revenue | (A) | ____ | ____ | ____ | ____ | ____ |
| Gross Margin | | ____ | ____ | ____ | ____ | ____ |
| Operating Expenses | (C) | ____ | ____ | ____ | ____ | ____ |
| Net Income | | ____ | ____ | ____ | ____ | ____ |
| | | | | | | |
| Base Revenue | ____ | ____ | ____ | ____ | ____ | ____ |
| Incremental Revenue | ____ | ____ | ____ | ____ | ____ | ____ |

**Figure 6–2.** Division scorecard.

Corporate Financial Scorecard (Corporate Income Statement)

| | Prior Mo. Actual | Current Month | | | % Variance | YTD | | | % Variance | Next Mo. Budget |
|---|---|---|---|---|---|---|---|---|---|---|
| | | Actual | Budget | Variance | | Actual | Budget | Variance | | |
| Customer Revenue | | | | | | | | | | |
|   Billed Revenue | | | | | | | | | | |
|   Discounts | | | | | | | | | | |
|   TOTAL CUST. REV. | | | | | | | | | | |
| Revenue Adjustments | | | | | | | | | | |
|   Billing Adjustments | | | | | | | | | | |
|   Bad Debt | | | | | | | | | | |
|   TOTAL REV. ADJ. | (1) | | | | | | | | | |
| Net Revenue | | | | | | | | | | |
| Cost of Revenue | | | | | | | | | | |
|   Access | | | | | | | | | | |
|   Directory Assistance | | | | | | | | | | |
|   Operator Services | | | | | | | | | | |
|   Product Sales | | | | | | | | | | |
|   TOTAL COST OF REV. | (2) | | | | | | | | | |
| Gross Margin | (3) | | | | | | | | | |
|   Direct Expenses | | | | | | | | | | |
|   Depreciation | | | | | | | | | | |
|   Corporate Allocations | | | | | | | | | | |
|   TOTAL OPER. EXP. | (4) | | | | | | | | | |
| Net Income | (5) | | | | | | | | | |
| Net Inc. as % of Cust. Rev. | | | | | | | | | | |

Division Scorecard (Division Financial Indicators)

| | Actual | Budget | Variance | Next Month Forecast | End of Year | |
|---|---|---|---|---|---|---|
| | | | | | Forecast | Variance |
| Net Revenue | (1) | | | | | |
| Cost of Revenue | (2) | | | | | |
| Gross Margin | (3) | | | | | |
| Operating Expenses | (4) | | | | | |
| Net Income | (5) | | | | | |
| Base Revenue | | | | | | |
| Incremental Revenue | | | | | | |

**Figure 6–3.** Corporate financial scorecard.

accountability. Each team's contributions are linked to and can be analyzed with its scorecard. A sample of team scorecards (Figure 6–2) consists of performance drivers in the Proposal Management, Customer Satisfaction, Order Processing, and Administrative areas. Figure 6–3 shows how each team and division performance has a direct cause-and-effect relationship with overall company performance. (Note that only some of the relationships are shown in this example.)

With the exception of the Administrative scorecard, the measures making up the performance drivers are not in dollars. They are comprised of the activities in each area that have an impact on the financial performance of the company. They are connected to tasks that employees perform each day. These scorecards provide a real-time view of employee performance and a means for individuals to see how the work they do ties into the bottom line of the company. They provide line-of-sight.

The concept of line of sight simply means that each company employee can see which line(s) on the financial statements they directly and indirectly affect. Some positions are easier than others, such as sales, production, and delivery. Other so-called support positions are less obvious, but with some analysis and cause-and-effect thinking, those employees classified as "overhead" discover where their value-added is.

The scorecards also provide a basis for discussion at the Huddles. For example, the Order Processing team has an established goal for percent of orders entered within three hours. They will discuss how they performed relative to that goal and depending on the results, will determine required corrective action if the target was missed or a plan to sustain and improve on performance if the goal was met. In addition, this target has a direct correlation to the "percent customer want dates met" goal within the Customer Satisfaction team.

As the departmental or team scorecards are rolled up into the division financial indicators, the business driver data is converted into dollar measures. The cost system that the cost accountants have managed and perfected over the years is the essence of this roll-up. In open-book companies, what the cost accountants know, everybody knows—at least in part. The cost of the service or the product—its component labor, and material and overhead—becomes a working number for the department or team.

In most companies, labor costs are a significant contributor to overall expenses. To forecast headcount additions or reductions can provide a critical piece to the financial results of the organization. A revenue-and-expense (including salary, training, travel, etc.) per head scorecard can help the department manage the hiring, training, and travel financial measures, providing the line-of-sight connection from the various budget items to the income statement.

At Boeing, the supervisors are taught discounted cash flow techniques, tools of the trade in managerial and cost accounting, so they can make intelligent choices about buy or make decisions, or about capital investments. These are more sophisticated analyses than many companies have yet to spread to their supervisors. But Boeing's goal is the same as any beginning open-book company, to help create the scorecards for increasing business literacy of all workers. Front-line scorecards are the first step in tying activity to bottom line results. The next step is to then connect the division performance, or division scorecards, to the overall company's results and scorecards.

In the Huddles, everyone who influences the company's success intensely scrutinizes business performance and results in detail. And they collectively look forward—each team predicts how it will do in the next 30, 60, 90 days against the goals or standards it has committed to achieve.

### ☑ SURVEY

Our open-book practices survey shows that most respondents see themselves as deficient in mastering information flow (Figure 6-4). Only 16 percent of the companies rated themselves high on establishing well-defined two-way communication systems. Sixty-nine percent rated themselves average (scoring themselves 4 to 7 on a scale of 1 to 10). The remaining 15 percent scored themselves low. It is critical to remember that resources put into financial education *will be lost* if Huddles—integrated information-rich communication processes—aren't also designed into the open-book practice set.

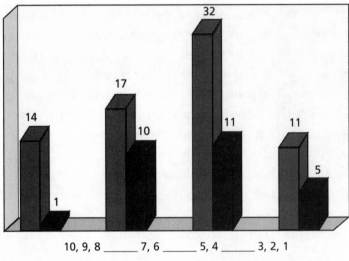

10, 9, 8 _____ 7, 6 _____ 5, 4 _____ 3, 2, 1

| 10 = Information, financial and other stays with upper management. | 1 = Information flows to employees through well-defined communication system and up to management on forecasted results against plan. |
|---|---|

| ■ Companies 100 – employees | ■ Companies 100 + employees |
|---|---|
| 14 | 1 |
| 17 | 10 |
| 32 | 11 |
| 11 | 5 |

**Figure 6–4.** Intensive Huddle System practices of forecasting numbers.

## INFORMATION IN REAL TIME

Most companies, big and small, are on information overload. In every company across the globe, businesspeople face daily, if not hourly, challenges related to getting the right information within the right time frame. Precisely to this point, the life blood, source of fuel for the Huddle System is *information in real time*—in time for it to be used by the *right* people to make the *right* decisions, helping the organization reach its objectives.

Necessary information comes from outside the company as well as from the various groups and teams within the organization. Information from outside pertains to trends and changes in the local and global economy, activities within the industry, specific competitor activity, and customer activity. Data and information from within the organization pertains to financial performance, the effective and efficient use of resources, the internal environment or culture.

Figures 6–5 and 6–6 outline and summarize the different types of information available to a company, their probable sources, and provides an example of how the information can be applied. Using as a lens your company's "big picture" goals, each team can create its own schema of critical numbers corresponding real-time information it needs to affect those numbers.

| A. Trends and shifts in Economy, National and International | |
|---|---|
| *Sources of Information* | *Application* |
| • Board of Directors<br>• CEO<br>• President<br>• CFO & Financial Managers | • Mostly long-term influence Prepares employees to participate in year to year planning and in strategic thinking, analysis and decision making. |

| B. Industry shifts and trends | |
|---|---|
| *Sources of Information* | *Application* |
| • Board of Directors<br>• CEO & President<br>• CFO, Controller<br>• Sales & Marketing<br>• Operations, Engineering<br>• Research & Development<br>• Customer Service | • Short- and long-term planning<br>• Decisions about immediate use of resources<br>• Decisions to change current strategies and tactics |

| C. Competitive activities | |
|---|---|
| *Sources of Information* | *Application* |
| • President<br>• Sales & Marketing<br>• Customer Service<br>• Product & Service Developers | • Short-term planning<br>• Decisions re: sales and marketing<br>• Customer service needs |

| D. Customers | |
|---|---|
| *Sources of Information* | *Application* |
| • Sales Manager<br>• Sales & Marketing<br>• Customer Service<br>• Other teams with customer contact or information (e.g., operations)<br>• Receptionist | • Short-term planning<br>• Decisions re: service, quality |

**Figure 6–5.** Information from external environment.

---

**A. Efficiency: Doing things right**

| *Sources of Information* | *Application* |
| --- | --- |
| • Front-line performers<br>• Support personnel<br>• Team leaders & middle managers<br>• Internal customer/supplier teams<br>• Engineering<br>• Purchasing<br>• Accounting & financial services | • Decisions re: resources and assets<br>• Business planning<br>• Influence of suppliers or customers on the business<br>• Process improvement |

**B. Effectiveness: Doing the right thing**

| *Sources of Information* | *Application* |
| --- | --- |
| • Human resources<br>• Front line performers<br>• Quality team<br>• Engineering<br>• Support staff<br>• Project leaders<br>• Sales<br>• Accounting & finance | • Assessment of asset utilization and other performance indicators<br>• Human resource management, planning, training<br>• Measure of teamwork capabilities<br>• Decision-making processes<br>• Organization design and structure |

**C. Financial Performance**

| *Sources of Information* | *Application* |
| --- | --- |
| • Sales<br>• Operations<br>• Manufacturing & distribution<br>• Purchasing<br>• Finance & accounting | • Short- and long-term planning<br>• Decisions re: resource utilization<br>• Assessment of organizations performance<br>• Feedback tool for all performers |

**D. Climate/Culture**

| *Sources of Information* | *Application* |
| --- | --- |
| • Leaders and managers<br>• Human resources<br>• All participants in the organization | • Expressed corporate values<br>• Early indicators for communication and team issues and concerns<br>• Growth opportunities<br>• Reward and recognition systems |

---

**Figure 6–6.** Information from internal environment.

**HANDS-ON
LESSONS**

## Encouraging Business Thinking versus Departmental Thinking

To help employees see their work's impact within the chain of the company's interlocking tasks and performance outcomes, use a worksheet like the one in Figure 6–7. Each team identifies and lists its critical performance measures in the middle column. Participants then think about, discuss, and ultimately identify the critical information flows into and out of their tasks. This helps employees get a picture and appreciate the value of interdependent cause-and-effect activities. Individuals, teams, and departments begin to recognize their interface with other teams. They realize when they receive or supply information and performance data they are responsible for a precise hand-off where no steps are missed and no one drops the ball. Business thinking versus departmental thinking takes over and better understanding about what affects performance measures develops.

Think about your daily tasks. What are the measures that represent the output of your work? List your relevant job measures on the worksheet (for individual or team). On the left, fill in the source of data and information you depend on. On the right, identify those who rely on your information and performance.

What are the Critical Numbers for your company? How are your job or team numbers linked to the company's Critical Numbers?

| Department/Team Who Supplies Information & Performance Data | Performance Measures for My Job | Departments/Teams Who Need Your Information & Performance Outcomes |
|---|---|---|
|  |  |  |
|  |  |  |
|  |  |  |
|  |  |  |
|  |  |  |

**Figure 6–7.** Develop business links.

## The Links in the Huddle System at Syncrude

Most managers complain about attending too many meetings, robbing them of the time they need to do their work. The Huddle System shortens meeting time by making them efficient, creating a common language, separating problem solving from information sharing, and getting the right information to people when they need it.

Don de Guerre at Syncrude Canada, Ltd., led an effort in his company to redesign their governance system and saw how the Huddle System would improve initiatives already underway:

"Syncrude was developing a way of linking different levels of work in a hierarchy of functions, which was called a participative governance system. This system was intended to involve every employee, but was meeting with limited success. The notion of an intensive huddle system using balance scorecards provided a renewed impetus to make this stewardship system work. Each team would develop a line of sight to company business results such that every employee understood their contribution to Syncrude's critical numbers."

VOICES

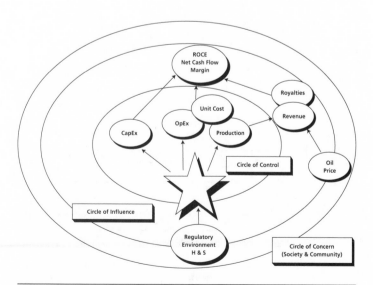

**Figure 6–8.** The influence diagram.

The conceptual framework used by Syncrude is depicted in their Influence Diagram in Figure 6–8. As Syncrude managers and teams further developed its Huddle Design, they produced a Team Ownership and Stewarding System (Figure 6–9) which identified the role of their managers, while incorporating the components of the action-based learning model

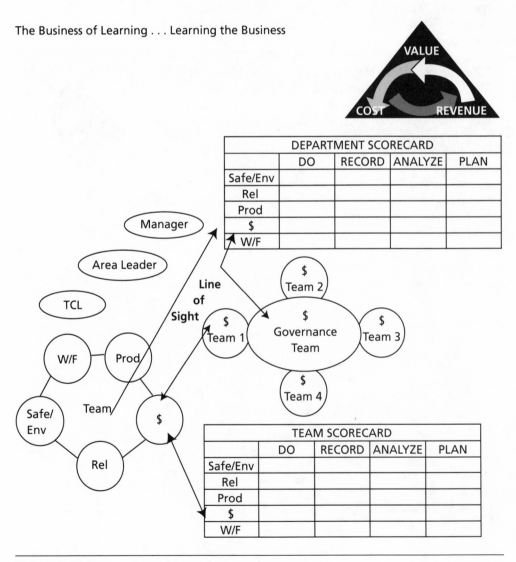

**Figure 6–9.** Team ownership and stewarding system.

the company had already established. The action-based learning model involves the four actions shown on the Team and Department scorecards: *Do, Record, Analyze, Plan.* The teams within a department roll up their performance results into a department scorecard as shown in Figure 6–9.

Information in the workplace flows in many different directions. Communication is often limited to taking care of the crises of the moment. Unless information is collected, systematically handed off, summarized, and made available to all in a just-in-time manner, its usefulness will be lessened or lost entirely to the enterprise at hand.

In many open-book companies, teams meet weekly to review current performances and to develop a 30- to 90-day outlook using their scorecards as points of reference. At Syncrude, the approach includes updates and discussions by managers who connected the current operational performance with their ROI goals, providing the link between the front-line and Syncrude's owner companies.

Using their costing system for calculating cost per barrel, a Syncrude critical number, each division—mining, extraction, upgrading, and power generation—tracks specific performance drivers such as overtime, downtime, and productivity per labor hour. With their learning system firmly in place, Syncrude managers continuously reinforce the connections between return on investment and cost per barrel of oil.

"We have taken every opportunity to give Syncrude's senior leaders updates on our key numbers and to discuss what they mean and how they're viewed by our owner companies and potential investors. This has enabled our managers to take this information and knowledge back into their teams to review it on a regular basis," says Phil Lachambra, CFO and vice president of business and corporate affairs.

**FIELD NOTES**

# Cultivating a High Level of Understanding at Web Converting

At Web Converting in Framingham, Massachusetts, the Film Team has a formal and advanced huddle system that links its production to customers and to specific revenue numbers. Here the team meetings are purposeful, targeted, and participative.

The Film Team Production Comparison Reports shown in Figures 6–10 and 6–11 shows the huddling team results in real-time of efforts against projected goals. Each work team's Huddle is a place of accountability and learning. Machine operator and team leader Rob Zicaro explains:

AUG 96

| | SALES NEEDED PER MONTH | SALES NEEDED PER DAY |
|---|---|---|
| PROJECTED SALES FOR THE MONTH OF **AUGUST** | $500,000 | $22,727 |
| BREAKEVEN SALES FOR THE MONTH = | 450,000 | 20,455 |
| ESOP CONTRIBUTION AMOUNT = | 30,000 | |
| BREAK-EVEN PLUS ESOP CONTRIBUTION FOR **AUGUST** | $480,000 | $21,818 |
| NUMBER OF WORKING DAYS IN THE MONTH = | 22 | |

| DATE: AUGUST | Projected Sales/Day | Break-Even Sales/Day | ON TIME | LATE | Break-Even ESOP Sales/Day | Production Report Value MTD | Actual Production Per Day | Today's Total Labor Hours | Today's Labor Rate |
|---|---|---|---|---|---|---|---|---|---|
| 1 | $ 22,727 | $ 20,455 | 2 | 0 | $ 21,818 | $ 23,900 | $ 23,900 | 375 | $63.73 |
| 2 | 45,455 | 40,909 | 4 | 0 | 43,636 | 44,011 | 20,111 | 306 | 65.72 |
| 5 | 68,182 | 61,364 | 1 | 2 | 65,455 | 65,022 | 21,011 | 376 | 55.88 |
| 6 | 90,909 | 81,818 | 6 | 0 | 87,273 | 88,162 | 23,140 | 376 | 61.54 |
| 7 | 113,636 | 102,273 | 6 | 0 | 109,091 | 108,554 | 20,392 | 376 | 54.23 |
| 8 | 136,364 | 122,727 | 1 | 4 | 130,909 | 128,949 | 20,395 | 376 | 54.24 |
| 9 | 159,091 | 143,182 | 3 | 2 | 152,727 | 151,500 | 22,551 | 341 | 66.13 |
| 12 | 181,818 | 163,636 | 6 | 2 | 174,545 | 176,500 | 25,000 | 356 | 70.22 |
| 13 | 204,545 | 184,091 | 3 | 1 | 196,364 | 201,021 | 24,521 | 356 | 68.88 |
| 15 | 250,000 | 225,000 | | | | | | | |
| 16 | 272,727 | 245,455 | | | | | | | |
| 19 | 295,455 | 265,909 | | | | | | | |
| 20 | 318,182 | 286,364 | | | | | | | |
| 21 | 340,909 | 306,818 | | | | | | | |
| 22 | 363,636 | 327,273 | | | | | | | |
| 23 | 386,364 | 347,727 | | | | | | | |
| 26 | 409,091 | 368,182 | | | | | | | |
| 27 | 431,818 | 388,636 | | | | | | | |
| 28 | 454,545 | 409,091 | | | | | | | |
| 29 | 477,273 | 429,545 | | | | | | | |
| 30 | 500,000 | 450,000 | | | | | | | |

22   # Of Days In AUGUST          Average Production Per Day =   $ 22,336          Average Labor Rate/Day = $62.29

ACTUAL TOTAL SALES FOR THE MONTH OF  AUGUST          =   $201,021

Amount Remaining to Reach Break-Even for:          MONTH TO DATE ON TIME % = 74.42%

| $298,979 | $248,979 | 32 | 11 | $278,979 |
|---|---|---|---|---|
| Projected Sales | Break-Even Sales | TOTAL ON TIME | TOTAL LATE | Break-Even Esop Sales |

**Figure 6–10.** Production comparison report.

| Film Team Projected Sales | Film Team Breakeven Sales | Customers | Invoiced Sales from Other Accts. | Labor Hours | Rate Per Labor Hour |
|---|---|---|---|---|---|
| $300,016 | $ 194,500 | ABC Corp. | $ 67,888 | | |
| | | Mass Port | $ 72,111 | | |
| | | Wilson | $ 14,994 | | |
| | | Jordan Marsh | $ 32,323 | | Rate Per Labor Hour |
| | | Par-Moore | $ 52,001 | Labor Hours | |
| | | All Others | $ 22,500 | | |
| | *Estimated* | Top-Acct. | $ 73,016 | 417 | $175.10 |
| Total Sales Other Than DuPont | | | $ 261,817 | 2,818 | $ 92.91 |
| Total Sales for the Team | | | $ 334,833 | 3,235 | $103.50 |

Film Team Production Report

Top-Acct. 22%
ABC Corp. 20%
All Others 7%
Mass Port 21%
Par-Moore 16%
Jordan Marsh 10%
Wilson 4%

**Figure 6–11.** Film team production comparison report.

**VOICES**

"We are building understanding and learning into the process of open-book management as we spin off individual work-team income statements from the plant's income statement. There are five teams, each representing a different type of service. These team income statements allow us to measure how each unit of our business is performing with respect to profitability, sales, contribution margin, direct labor hours, and revenue per hour. The team income statements are the first level of financial insight for our front-line people, illustrating how their team's financial performance fits into the plant's financial success. This begins the process of narrowing the scope of direct activities that move the financial levers within our business. This meeting also serves as a forum for communicating business initiatives, such as ISO 9002 advancements, total quality principles, and new business opportunities for our plant.

The perspective of the big picture is addressed at our monthly meeting, when the whole plant shuts down to review the income statement from the previous month. One purpose of the meeting is to analyze the three-page profit-and-loss statement sharing the finances of the plant and highlighting any differences, positive or negative, in the categories of sales, cost-of-goods sold, payroll, operating expenses, profits or losses, and revenue per hour. Comparisons of year-to-date averages, and previous month's performance, are also taken into account as we review the statement line by line. It's not uncommon for a front-line person to lead this part of the meeting as we examine the month's financial performance. For a peer to stand up and explain the numbers adds a realness to the process and makes it less intimidating for all of us. Questions are always encouraged and any item not understood is explained in basic terms and concepts, which builds a shared understanding."

## Fun, $50s and Financial Literacy at Foldcraft

**FIELD NOTES**

At Foldcraft, the department and production teams meet weekly to focus on their portion of the pie, knowing that it will all be pulled together before their eyes every month. Steve Sheppard, CEO of Foldcraft Company, says a high level of maturity and understanding has developed in his company over the course of six years of open-book practice:

"Foldcraft conducts its monthly huddle, wherein the income statements for the current month and the next two forward are built in front of all 250 members of the organization. For the one-hour session, we're divided up into our units, each with its own colors and signs of identity. We ask quiz questions which, when answered correctly, are worth $50 to the first respondent. We give money for questions asked by nonmanagers or answered by nonmanagers. We talk openly about what's going on in the firm. The senior managers wear referee jerseys and carry whistles to ensure that the kinds of comments and questions are appropriate and not offensive to anyone. (We haven't had to throw a flag yet!) And the last financial question, pass or play in front of the entire audience, is worth a crisp $100 bill when answered correctly! How else can you account for a woodworker knowing the worker's compensation modification rating for 1996?"

VOICES

## Open-Book Variance Analysis at Sprint

Mary Hansen spent 15 years in finance and accounting at Sprint in Kansas City, Missouri. In 1993, she was part of the open-book management implementation team in Sprint's Government Systems Division. She describes the shift that took place in the accounting group with open-book practices:

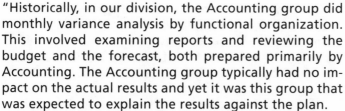

FIELD NOTES

"Historically, in our division, the Accounting group did monthly variance analysis by functional organization. This involved examining reports and reviewing the budget and the forecast, both prepared primarily by Accounting. The Accounting group typically had no impact on the actual results and yet it was this group that was expected to explain the results against the plan.

Within the implementation of OBM, it soon became evident to those in our division that this was backwards. It makes much more sense to have employees analyze their own variances by looking at the internal and external drivers in their piece of the business. It is their activity that has created the actual results. Who else would better know the numbers?

VOICES

**HANDS-ON
LESSONS**

## Key Questions and Factors in Designing Your Huddle System

To start the design of your Huddle System, you'll have to take the following factors into consideration:

- Your current meeting system.
- Ways that data is collected and transferred internally.
- Number of company locations.
- The amount of time currently invested in meetings.
- The important points of interface between critical tasks and workflows.
- The capability of your computer technology.

Keeping in mind the need to connect information with people, while maintaining a big picture focus and linking performance measures to financial results, determine the following:

- Which performance drivers such as quality, customer satisfaction, proposals submitted, have the most impact on desired companywide outcomes?
- Which teams own each performance driver and should track it?
- How does each team's performance affect others?
- How can the performance factors be translated into financial numbers? By whom?

Using the chart in Figure 6–12 as a guide, determine the specific performance measures that teams, departments, and divisions at your company should huddle around.

When scorecards are developed, teams can and should use them regularly. Next, connect, in a roll-up design, team performance to department performance, to division performance, to the company's financial performance. These connections often consist of linking various components of performance drivers as illustrated at the beginning of Chapter 5 (Figures 5–2 and 5–3).

Finally, determine how you'll account for the current big picture performance of your company and provide the outlook for the performance of the next 30, 60, 90 days. If you are a small enough company or division that operates in one location, you can combine the main and post huddles.

| Pre-Huddles | Main Huddle | Post-Huddles |
|---|---|---|
| Focus:<br>• Review performance scorecards<br>• Current activities reported<br>• Variance analysis<br>• Predict probable outcomes<br>• Prep for Main Huddle<br>• Assign corrective action<br>• Teach<br>• Learn | Focus:<br>• Sales trends for the next months.<br>• All functions tied together.<br>• Review past performance against plan.<br>• Problems identified (not solved).<br>• Business analysis via numbers.<br>• Forecast for next month reviewed and updated.<br>• Company and individual activities and interests. | Focus:<br>• Precise relay of information data shared in main huddle.<br>• Accountabilities reviewed and assigned.<br>• Teach<br>• Learn |
| Who: Small teams of two or more in functional units of between functions/departments. | Who: Representatives from each function. | Who: Each department or team or function. |
| When: Some daily, some weekly, as needed. | When: Weekly or monthly. | When: Weekly and within 24 hours of Main Huddle. |
| Tools: Charts, scorecards, reports, work orders. | Tools: Monthly income statement, cash flow statement and other financial tools as needed. | Tools: Income Statement, cash flow and other financials as needed. |
| Where: Anywhere—lunch room, shopfloor, over the internet. | Where: Conference room, video or phone conference. | Where: In a department or local meeting room, phone conference. |
| How Long: 10 min., 20 min., just long enough to take care of business. | How Long: 60 to 90 minutes. | How Long: 30 to 60 minutes. |
| Leader: Manager of Team Leader. | Leader: President or alternate. | Leader: Team Leader and person who attended main huddle. |

**Figure 6–12.** Intensive Huddle System components.

As a result, variance analysis now begins at the team level in the form of pre-Huddles. Teams or departments look at their performance drivers, the nonfinancial measures, as a start into explaining variances. For example, in Proposal Management, they look at the number of proposals outstanding, won, lost, active, and inactive. They determine what went right in winning a proposal and what went wrong if a proposal was lost. It's not just identifying a number but telling the story behind the number.

As variances are understood at the team level, they are then rolled up to a division level at the main Huddle."

In Figure 6–13, Mary Hansen outlines the differences between a more traditional approach and the open-book approach to variance analysis. As employees learn about the various drivers that influence the outcomes of their business—"currency fluctuation did

| Traditional | Open-Book Management |
|---|---|
| Few individuals outside of the Finance/accounting area understand the numbers that make up the business. | Critical numbers that make up the business are identified in each functional area to establish line of sight to overall financial performance. |
| Finance/accounting department prepares performance reporting that is used internally. | Finance/accounting department and different teams prepares performance reporting and distributes to functional areas of the organization. |
| Finance/accounting department performs analysis of actual results to budget and forecast. | Each functional area reviews its own actual results to determine the reasons for variances to the budget and forecast. |
| Finance/accounting department provides explanations of variances to other functional areas in the organization. | Each individual functional area provides explanations of variances to the organization during the main huddle. |
| Functional areas are not held accountable for variances. | Functional areas are expected to not only understand variances but are held accountable for any action required as a result of the differences. |
| Variance information, for the most part, is not used in the decision-making process. | Variance information is an integral part of the decision-making process, in planning strategy, determining corrective action, and revising the forecast. |
| Variance information, for the most part, is not tied to the "big picture" of the organization including changes in the business and environment. | To make accurate use of variance information, each functional area determines other functions that could have influenced the numbers and communicates with those groups in the overall scope of the business. |

**Figure 6–13.** Variance analysis.

*that* to our profits?"—they adjust their perspective and expand their understanding of how they fit and contribute. And as teams analyze the variances having to do with their performance measures, they become knowledgeable enough to determine how their variance affects other functions as well as financial results.

Teaching employees to analyze their performance variances and to understand the explanations of big picture variances means they need to develop two areas of business-specific knowledge:

First, they need to understand how actions, behaviors, or "drivers" determine a financial number. For example, the sales number might be influenced by internal operations as illustrated in Mary Hansen's example:

**VOICES**

"When revenue is less than expected, the vice president of sales huddles with the order entry group to determine if there is a backlog of new orders that has delayed installation and the start of billing. He asks if there is a problem with the quality of the orders. He huddles with the group responsible for installing service to determine if there are problems there. He huddles with customer service to find out if customers are dissatisfied for some reason. He huddles with accounting to see if there are problems with getting revenue recorded to the general ledger. He huddles with the information services group to ensure no systems problems.

In other words, he steps out of his corner of the world into other areas of the larger world. He is not looking at just dollar figures. He is looking at the business drivers, the events behind the dollars. He wants to understand the month's activity so he can understand the impact of the nonfinancial measures on the revenue number."

Second, they must understand how external conditions can affect performance measures. The economy has an impact on the price a company pays to produce and deliver its products or services, how much customers will buy, or the interest rate the company will pay if a loan is required. Even the weather is an externality that must be considered in planning for and in explaining variances, as Mary Hansen describes:

**VOICES**

"When a hurricane or tornado devastates a community, emergency service must be available for disaster relief teams. The company incurs millions of dollars in additional expense for repair crews to work around the clock restoring service. If people cannot make telephone calls, revenue is lost.

A few years ago a switch site was flooded during a heavy rain. A significant number of customers were affected by the outage. There were customer contracts in place that were specific about service availability so the

**HANDS-ON LESSONS**

---

## Teach Variance Analysis and Improve Line-of-Sight Vision

1. Identify the specific components that go into making up your performance measures. Distinguish for your team which of the components are fixed and which tend to vary and why.
2. Identify the external drivers (influencing factors) that have impact on your measures. If it is appropriate, assign "lookout" duty for each driver to different members of the team. For example, several can watch competitor activity, others can watch segments of customer activity, and so on.
3. Link variance analysis with line of sight to the income statement. Start with parts of the income statement that most represent your company's performance. If, for example, 60 percent of your costs are in salaries and benefits, as can be the case in a professional services company, highlight this number. Then teach the major factors that cause those costs to vary, such as a customer requiring more time than is in the contract, or unanticipated meetings to fulfill a contract requirement.
4. Focus on the impact of customer retention. Those in marketing and customer service will be surprised to see how they directly reduce costs by retaining a customer versus acquiring a new one.

company had to determine when billing adjustments were warranted. It had a real impact on both revenues and expenses that had been unforeseen in the planning process."

## Open-Book Style Project Management at HSM Group

In professional service companies such as engineering and consulting, the use of variance analysis and the concept of line of sight can be applied to project management. The principle is fundamental: Focus on what is most controllable in your type of business. In a manufacturing company, it can make sense, as Web Converting's Rob Zicaro has illustrated, to create an income statement for each team that rolls into the plant income statement every month. Service companies can do the same thing by focusing on individual projects and rolling them up.

**FIELD NOTES**

Judy Friefield, controller at the HSM Group, a service research and marketing firm serving health care providers explains her company's approach:

"As a small service company, we have faced the challenge of adjusting the Huddle concept to something that is meaningful and workable for us. Our Huddle System is still undergoing major refinements. We have found that some of the concepts used by others have little meaning for us, as a small consulting firm. We currently have a weekly Huddle at a standard time. Once a month, we discuss the status and profitability of our projects and once a month we review the previous month's financial statements and progress toward our goals. The remaining two weekly Huddles are for general items or issues of concern."

**VOICES**

Figure 6–14 illustrates how HSM captures the revenues and associated costs for each project. Note that it is capturing both direct and indirect labor to get a true picture of the profitability for each of its projects. This scorecard is used by HSM project teams and keeps everyone, professionals and support staff alike, accountable for results.

Client Project:          **Total Contract Amount:**     **$22,000.00**
Job:        **MARKETING EFFORT FOR**
Project Mgr:   **JOAN**

| USER | MGMT | RESEARCH | WRITE | CONSULT | MEETINGS | SECRETARY | G&A | TOTAL $ |
|------|------|----------|-------|---------|----------|-----------|-----|---------|
| ANN | 59.06 | | | | | | | 59.06 |
| ARIELLA | 156.18 | 34.23 | 152.10 | | | | | 342.51 |
| JOAN | 324.82 | | | | | | 9.84 | 334.66 |
| SUE | | 82.68 | | | | 55.12 | 17.23 | 155.03 |
| TRISH | 45.56 | | 28.48 | | | | | 74.04 |
| | 585.62 | 116.91 | 180.58 | 0.00 | 0.00 | 55.12 | 27.07 | 965.30 |

| Project Variance Analysis | Actual Labor | Budgeted Labor | Variance | - % - | Actual Costs | Budgeted Costs | Variance | - % - |
|---------------------------|--------------|----------------|----------|-------|--------------|----------------|----------|-------|
| | 965.30 | 3593.00 | 2627.70 | 73.13 | 11.10 | 7700.00 | 7688.90 | 99.86 |

**Figure 6–14.** HSM Group Ltd. project job cost summary.

In a service business, the amount of direct labor required to fulfill a client's need may exceed the amount allocated to the project pricing, and turn the project into a loser. Friefield says team contributors are seeing their roles differently because they have seen the importance of predicting their project costs accurately:

**VOICES**

"We have seen dramatic changes in our employees' attitudes and their sense of ownership. We have seen employees at all levels take the initiative to reduce operating expenses and look for more efficient ways to work. They now know each decision affects their personal pocketbooks, not just the company's bottom line. The other day a consultant was working on a proposal and said to me that last year she would not have fought for increasing the professional fees to the level that she knew was necessary to do the job in a quality way and profitably. She would have done a wonderful job and expected a good bonus for her work. Today,

| TRAVEL | ADMIN | PRINTING | PRODUCT | RESEARCH | MISC | TOTAL EXP | |
|--------|-------|----------|---------|----------|------|-----------|---|
| | | | | | | 0.00 | |
| | | | | | | 0.00 | |
| | | | | | | 0.00 | |
| | | | | | 11.10 | 11.10 | |
| | | | | | | 0.00 | |
| | | | | | | | **TOTAL COSTS** |
| 0.00 | 0.00 | 0.00 | 0.00 | 0.00 | 11.10 | 11.10 | 976.40 |
| | | | | | | TOTAL BILLED | 22000.00 |
| | | | | | CONTRIBUTION TO OVERHEAD | | 21023.60 |
| | | | | | OVERHEAD (38%) | | 8360.00 |
| | | | | | PROFIT/(LOSS) | | 12663.60 |
| | | | | | PCT COMPLETE | | % |
| | | | | | PCT BILLED | | 100% |

because of OBM, she is fighting to put the "right" number in the proposal, because her bonus is tied to the company's profitability. This message is not an isolated situation. I hear these things all the time; and therefore, I can tell that the concept of OBM is hard at work."

## Everyone Has a Line-of-Sight: Finding and Filling Potholes at Capital Connections

Line-of-sight can be established for anyone at any level of the company, directly revealing that person's economic impact. Even people in so-called support positions—usually classified as overhead—can see where their added value is. The process can be enlightening—and fun. At Capital Connections, for example, when we saw our administrative expenses trending upward over several months, we assigned our administrative staff the job of analyzing the negative variance. If need be, they were to create a scorecard system to help us get on top of the escalating expenses.

**FIELD NOTES**

Like many growth companies, we have a fast-paced business environment. Our focus is to react to client needs and potential business as a priority. In the process, we can lose the details. What Cindy Hicks and Debra Neel discovered for us in their analysis was an expensive problem with shipping. Books, brochures, sample business literacy quizzes, and other materials were going out the door or over the fax so fast that our overnight delivery expenses had grown exponentially. Some of it, had we been tracking and capturing it carefully, was billable to the client, other parts were a marketing expense, still others belonged to project management or administrative expense.

We now use the *Shipping Scorecard* shown in Figure 6–15. Cindy and Debra, who had been with us just over three months, made a real contribution to the business. They now look out for other potential expense potholes. Cindy summed it up, "I had no idea it could be this much fun."

## Open-Book Evolution: From Reporting to Forecasting at AQP

**FIELD NOTES**

At the Association for Quality and Participation (AQP)—whose 25 staff members and active chapters throughout the country support over 10,000 members—a long history of open information and empowering employees lead them to open-book practices before other companies and surely before other associations. Executive director Cathy Kramer and her team have led the association through the heady days when the Baldrige award was piquing interest and everybody wanted to attend a conference on quality, to the sober days of a highly competitive conference market.

Though AQP is not-for-profit, increased competition nevertheless means more attention to the numbers. Amy Katz, AQP's head of research and educational programs, joined Cathy Kramer in articulating why AQP needed to become an open-book environment:

**VOICES**

"The headquarters staff of the Association for Quality and Participation is dedicated to living out the principles of quality and participation which we promote. We believe that a successful organization is one that has a highly involved, competent, and committed workforce, one that is satisfying the customers, and one that is enjoying healthy returns through effective

MONTH: _____

| Client or Project | Type of Delivery | Amount | Billable Amount | Total Cost |
|---|---|---|---|---|
| | | | | |
| | | | | |
| | | | | |
| | | | | |
| | | | | |

**Figure 6–15.** Shipping scorecard.

use of internal resources and keen marketplace analysis. How should an organization be designed to produce this kind of success? A key strategy for us is that all staff must be financially and organizationally literate. By this we mean that everyone must understand the economics of the department in which they work as well as the AQP as a whole. They must also be literate about the business realities in which we operate. They are expected to know who our major customers are, who our competitors are, and the major trends in the field of quality and participation, and the business world which we are trying to influence."

AQP's open-book efforts revolve around the plan that the board puts in place and the budget that derives from the plan. After each department puts together its budget, all employees get an opportunity to ask questions and give input. The process is reiterated until the budget is set for conferences, programs, membership, product sales, the journal, and advertising. Then the new fiscal and program year begins with the plan in everybody's heads, not necessarily agreeing with every line item, but having had a chance to be heard.

Listen to Kramer and Katz as they describe their open-book evolution—going from a report of what was past to a *forecasting* process:

**VOICES**

"For years, we distributed financial statements to all staff every month. We have discovered a number of problems with this: (1) the 5- to 7-page financials are probably too much information for some; (2) the financials reflect history and so are simply a snapshot of the work in the past. The financials are simply numbers without the context of sales predicted (except in a general sense as reflected in the annual budget), and expenses that were predicted to occur in a certain month may have been postponed, reallocated, or saved.

We now produce a forecast each month to address these concerns. Each product owner projects future revenue and expenses for the year. These are discussed in monthly state-of-the-business meetings, which are open to all staff. Here we look at the big picture—how we're doing at meeting our annual commitments, as well as looking for ways to optimize each product through system improvements and recognizing interdependencies. The Huddle approach to reviewing and forecasting numbers is intriguing though it's been hard to institute that given the seasonal nature of our business. Because we are small, we can also make our number commitments visible to all staff. We keep running totals for conference and education course attendance and membership numbers on a white board."

**FIELD NOTES**

## Predicting the Future at Web Converting

A substantial difference between traditional business management and open-book management—and one that is essential for effective Huddles—is the intense focus on projecting performance. Employees know that things change, but they don't always understand why they change. OBM lifts the fog and helps them understand why.

Equipped with the business finance knowledge, and the awareness of their line-of-sight, employees and managers can predict how close they will come to meeting their plan numbers and measures. Through the Huddle System, this all-important information is sent throughout the company so all the interdependent parts hear the information in real-time and can adjust their plans accordingly. Rob Zicaro's group at Web Converting has made an art form of this kind of predictive Huddling:

Voices

"Channelling information into our "roadmaps" allows each team to measure their daily performance against monthly projections. We use the term roadmap to describe each team's spreadsheet comparing monthly projections with actual performance in sales, on-time deliveries, revenue per hour, workdays-in-month, profits, and the break-even figure for the team. The roadmap forecasts the monthly business opportunities for each team. Everyday our actual performance is updated on the roadmaps. This information is posted in the team financial information center, providing immediate feedback for all members. These roadmaps are a real-time approach to impacting the finances of the plant as they unfold. The idea is to focus on the present financial performance instead of the historic results at the end of each month. The combination of revenue per hour figures and comparing actual financial performance against projected revenue targets, keeps our hands on the financial levers that move our business daily. In our morning Huddle, we review our updated roadmap along with the revenue per man-hour figures from the previous 24 hours of production. This information reflects where we are in the month and what jobs in progress need action to raise the revenue per hour figure."

Like the regular practice of any professional sports team, dance troupe, or performing arts group, the Huddle System is the practice field for business players. It is the place where each person challenges his or her teammates to perform better and responds to similar challenges. This peer-to-peer accountability is motivating and even ennobling. Here Zicaro's words inspiringly capture the human spirit of open-book accountability:

"Facilitating this process of financial focus each day breathes life into the numbers, making them come alive with the successes and challenges inherent in a company of businesspeople. It's important that our numbers have a human dimension and connection attached to them if we are to move them upward. People must know and believe they are able to do something about them through performance improvements and

Voices

work design. It's this kind of human connection that increases a company's competitive advantage within the marketplace and cultivates real financial security. This powerful human connection is a goal we constantly strive for as we continuously learn about the power of open-book management."

# 7

## No-Kidding Ownership

### Leveraging the
### Motivational Multiplier

*Most compensation systems are boring. Most do not pay for perfor-*
*mance. Few encourage commitment to the organization. And while they*
*can send powerful messages to employees about the kind of organization*
*they work for and the skills and behaviors it values, most of those mes-*
*sages—and systems—are uninspiring. In fact, they often inhibit organi-*
*zations and employees from achieving the highest levels of performance.*

Catharine Meek
President
Meek and Associates
Compensation Consulting Firm

*From the 1980s through the 1990s, inflation-adjusted incomes grew*
*strongly only at the top. Income growth was sluggish in middle brackets*
*and dropped in lower segments. That's in sharp contrast to the 1960s*
*and 1970s when a strong economy boosted all income segments.*

*USA Today*
August 22, 1996

It was a good bargain while it
worked. And it worked for a long time. "We'll pay you
just enough to make it worth your while not to quit,"
said management. "Ok, we'll work just hard enough
to make it worth your while not to fire us," responded
the workforce. That was the Faustian bargain that

dominated compensation thinking for decades. The enterprise provided the workforce with minimal pay, for which it received minimal effort.

Journalist Studs Terkel captured the essence of this bargain in his stark and not-so-uplifting *Working*, a 1972 chronicle of working Americans. The book opens with the voice of Mike Lefevre, a steel worker in Cicero, "You can't take pride any more. It's hard to take pride in a bridge you're never gonna cross, in a door you're never gonna open. You're mass-producing things and you never see the end result of it. How are you gonna get excited about pullin' steel?"

It was an okay bargain, not uplifting but at least predictable. And many workers did fine as long as purchasing power and wages went up. There was no need for open books, incentive-based compensation, or reward and recognition systems. Management wasn't particularly interested in workers' ideas for improving the business anyway. Most employees didn't expect work to be stimulating or exciting, and many looked for meaning and fun elsewhere, in their family, community, church, or synagogue.

In case you haven't noticed, *things have changed*. Declines in real wages over the past decade and a half have made the old bargain untenable for workers (Figure 7–1). Increased competitive pressures on all

| 1966–1979 | | | | |
| --- | --- | --- | --- | --- |
| Top 1/5th | | | | Bottom 1/5th |
| 23% | 22% | 20% | 15% | 16% |

| 1966–1979 | | | | |
| --- | --- | --- | --- | --- |
| Top 1/5th | | | | Bottom 1/5th |
| 17% | 8% | –1% | –5% | –13% |

USA Today

**Figure 7–1.** Dividing the income brackets into fifths.

business have left companies looking for ways to increase effectiveness and efficiency. There is a mad scramble to create incentive systems for all employees that link their efforts to shareholder value and to other long- and short-term financial and customer and market outcomes.

But for all the scrambling, there is still a long way to go.

Our contention—and the underlying theme of this chapter—is that the bonus system, as hard as it is to do well, is just the *beginning* of open-book management. When tied to line-of-sight financial know-how, and to accountable forecasting against a plan by teams, it becomes something many times more powerful. We call this *No-Kidding Ownership,* a set of practices that give employees *intrinsic* motivators—like task ownership, a sense of self-directedness and responsibility, team participation and feedback—as well as *extrinsic* motivators like recognition, rewards, and incentive-based compensation. This motivational blend gives workers a real stake in the outcome of their enterprise. It also makes work engaging, fun and *effective.*

In terms of compensation for work, the Western world had progressed from pure exploitation, to compensation, and, for some, to incentive awards, stock and more advanced forms of partnership. No-Kidding Ownership is another step forward. Most of the benefits, rewards, and pay practices applied generally to employees today used to be reserved as executive perks. In time, they trickled down to the rest of the workforce as a set of recruiting and motivational tools. Each of the features has its own history, like sick leave or health benefits. (Most Americans who can remember the good old days of more affordable health care are painfully aware of the recent history of health care bennies.) The *general trend* of bonuses, incentivized pay, is outlined in Figure 7–3.

## ☑ SURVEY

The survey conducted by Capital Connections asked companies to rate themselves on a scale of 1 to 10, how far they had committed to open-book compensation practices. A 10 indicated that only senior management participates in bonus system, if there is one. A 1 indicated that all employees gain with improved financial performance through incentives and recognition systems. Figure 7–2 shows the results of the survey. Well over half of the respondents said their company had a bonus and variable pay system in which the accomplishment of financial goals directly affects employee paychecks. More than a third said *all* employees are included in the plan. Only 10 percent said that incentives

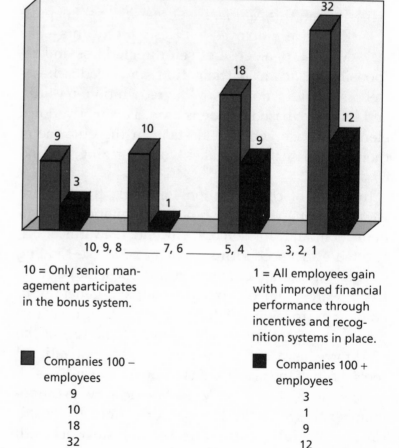

| 10, 9, 8 _____ 7, 6 _____ 5, 4 _____ 3, 2, 1 |

10 = Only senior management participates in the bonus system.

1 = All employees gain with improved financial performance through incentives and recognition systems in place.

■ Companies 100 − employees
9
10
18
32

■ Companies 100 + employees
3
1
9
12

**Figure 7–2.** No-kidding ownership practices of variable pay.

were for executives only. This represents a sea change over the last 10 years in compensation practices. In the early 1980s most employees across America (surveyed by Yankelovich and others) believed that when they worked harder and better someone else would get the payoff. Things are not that way anymore, for the companies in this survey, and we suspect for most others, as incentive pay has been on the rise.

No-Kidding Ownership pay and bonus practices inherently shrink the purchasing power gap that has been widening since the late 1970s because management makes a conscious decision to align its interests with those of nonmanagers. This component of business literacy philosophy—all employees learn to generate wealth and therefore all employees share in the gain—is a burgeoning movement that acts as a healthy

| Pay Element | Message |
|---|---|
| Base pay | Security. |
| Benefits | Guarantees. |
| Annual increases | No risk. |
| Managers always paid more than individual or technical contributors | Become a manager. |
| Incentives and perquisites are only for executives | Status and hierarchy are important. |
| Sales commission on volume only | Sales have no influence on margin. |
| Individual incentive emphasis | Teamwork is secondary. |
| Small incremental incentives | Incremental change, not entrepreneurial breakthroughs, is important. |

**Figure 7–3.** General trends.

counter trend to recent history of less purchasing power for the lower three-fifths of society.

Listen to Steve Sheppard describe the benefits he experiences from the investment Foldcraft has made and the essential role of establishing personal stakes in the outcome:

**VOICES**

"But the more tangible payoff, the one that our members look for more and more because of their new insights, is in the improvements to the operation, the money that is either saved or made as a direct result of their understanding and action. That's a light going on with dollar signs behind it! And that is meaningful to each member of the Company because of our 100 percent employee-owned status.

Employee ownership provides an ideal environment in which to teach people financial literacy, because in an ESOP (Employee Stock Ownership Plan) they are truly developing financial skills for their own benefit, whether long-term in stock appreciation or short-term through bonuses. Employee ownership itself was not a prerequisite for open-book management practice at Foldcraft. What was required, though, was a complete description of what benefits would be created for our members when we had performed more successfully through knowledge of the numbers. In other words, we had to be clear about what was in it for them, why they should go to the trouble of learning all of this new and previously forbidden information.

Thus, a portion of our earliest financial education included a thorough description of our short-term (quarterly) bonus program, a reorientation to the performance appraisal process that highlighted the performance value of knowing the critical numbers, and revisiting all of the other incentive programs in place at that time. In the case of Foldcraft, we also spent a great deal of time talking about stock values and equity ownership, but the key to member buy-in was understanding that there was something in it for them.

The reality is that there are many ESOP companies that have never attempted use of the open-book strategy and many non-ESOP companies that have motivated their members very well without the presence of stock acquisition. But whether in the form of stock, bonuses, incentive pay, companywide recognition, or some other benefit, people have to be able to see the reward in order to go after it."

Reward and compensation systems directly reflect the values of the managers and owners of the organization (Figure 7–4). No-Kidding Ownership is the system of systems for capturing the best energies of people by sending out the messages loud and strong that:

- We are all in this together, for the short- *and* the long-term.
- Financial rewards follow performance.
- Individual effort is recognized and rewarded.
- Lack of individual effort affects *everyone*.
- We can accomplish great goals and it can be *fun*.

If a company lags in employee excitement, it suffers from a compensation and reward system that is doing nothing to tap the latent heart and soul energies of its

| From | To |
| --- | --- |
| Discretionary | Predetermined by company |
| Strategy with managers only | Specific measures all employees |
| End of year | Frequent pay-out (quarterly or monthly) |
| Behavior-based | Results-based |
| Managers and employees separate plan | All employees on a same plan |
| Individual performance company and individual | Combination of team and performance |

**Figure 7–4.** Manager and owner values.

people. No-Kidding Ownership rests on the artful blend of several factors of human motivation:

- Extrinsic motivators: cash bonus, stock, and non-monetary rewards.
- Intrinsic motivators: joy of accomplishment, learning, being engaged.
- Competitive fire: the desire to surpass others as well as one's own limits.
- Need for autonomy: the desire to control one's own behavior, exert will.
- Need for teamwork: the desire to be part of something larger.

The best No-Kidding Ownership systems offer a variety of intrinsic and extrinsic stimulators. They allow a business literate work force to be *capable* of true partnership with management and shareholders.

## MANCO's Multimotivational Environment

**Field Notes**

MANCO is a No-Kidding Ownership motivational masterpiece, a $145 million producer of duct tape on the east side of Cleveland that competes successfully against a $300 million division of 3M. Its 300 plus employees have been singled out by *Inc.,* among others for the innovative way they do business.

MANCO is a creation of Jack Kahl, his two sons, and former COO Tom Korbo. Their motto "people do business with people" is what drives all their relationships with bankers, suppliers, distributors, customers—and with employees.

Kahl and the other leaders have made sure that the people at MANCO are motivated by learning, by their bonuses, by the ESOP, by wanting to surpass themselves, by the joy of work, by winning, excellence, and *fun:*

- *Learning:* Kahl is focused on what he calls the "learning speed" of the company and he has made the goal of more competence and knowledge a driver at MANCO. "The world is our classroom," is one of his pet aphorisms.

- *Achievement:* "We're not about to lose." Sounds like pre-Super Bowl bravado from a 240-pound linebacker, but it's how one female, silver-haired middle-aged MANCO-ite describes the customer service obsession instilled by Kahl. "We don't win if we don't help our customers win, the small ones just as much as the big ones like Kmart and Wal-Mart."

- *Monetary rewards:* MANCO is 30 percent employee-owned, and has a bonus tied to company results paid out at the end of the year. This yearly pay-out defies the pay-bonuses-frequently rule of thumb, but that just proves how powerful the intrinsic motivators are at MANCO.

- *Excellence and fun:* The intrinsic motivations of excelling and having fun are probably embodied in MANCO's two mascots. The champion racehorse Secretariat is an active symbol at MANCO, often evoked by Kahl and others in the company. It seems when the autopsy was done on the triple-crown winner, there was an amazing finding: Its heart was twice the size of that of the average thoroughbred. The inspiring horse set outrageous standards for excellence, once winning the Preakness by 33 lengths, a feat akin to winning the pennant by 40 games. Its symbolism for everyone at MANCO is obvious and palpable. Says Kahl, "MANCO is like Secretariat, a yearling with a big heart that loves to run. . . . Our job as managers is to put an "organized chaotic" plan in front of our people and let them run. This allows us to stay on target and innovate at the same time."

On the other side of the motivational coin, when you visit MANCO, a life-size duck (*duck* tape, get it?) shakes your hand and shows you around. At holiday time, you're likely to receive a card from MANCO featuring the yellow fellow. For employees and customers, the duck is anything but silly—it has become a symbol of the warm relationship MANCO has with its suppliers, customers, and community.

MANCO is filled with more spirit than most companies many times its size. It is a shining example of a primary No-Kidding Ownership teaching point for managers: *Whatever management does with incentives, it has to inspire.* It needs to get people excited about improvements and results. The excitement won't happen without constant communication by management to point out that the business is fun when the company and everyone in it wins.

## GM Invents a Better Measurement: RONA

For as long as most managers at GM can remember, earnings before interest and taxes (EBIT), was the mother of all measures. But as most people know, the big company got in some major trouble in the last auto recession and was slower than the others to turn around. GM was so slow that it became, in fact, a long-standing joke about bureaucracy.

The slumbering giant still had a few tricks up its sleeves, and its $6.9 billion in earnings in 1995 marked a turnaround the size of many economies. To make the turnaround less susceptible to the inevitable next recession GM decided to retire EBIT as its Holy Grail, replacing it with return on net assets (RONA). This represented a shift away from a single focus on earnings to one that measures earnings as related to utilized assets. RONA still rewards earnings, but it ties the managers to the balance sheet where all those assets are accounted for—some $220 billion.

And RONA carries with it the longer term outlook of wise capital investment, not just this year's or quarter's earnings. Shareholders hopefully would appreciate the broader measure, because a more balanced view can take the swings out of dividends and stock price fluctuations. In the old system, earnings could go up but RONA could go down. Managers could walk away with bonus checks even as the company's value declined.

CFO Michael Losh is quick to point out that RONA doesn't guarantee growth and critics of RONA say that it can drive short-term thinking, encouraging managers to put off sound capital investments and crippling the company later. But as anyone putting together an incentive plan will attest, no measure is risk-free and all need to be balanced. Losh sees RONA as the right measure to reward in today's environment:

"RONA represents an evolution. When you look at where GM needed to focus over the past couple of years, you see that we were coming through a classic turnaround situation. We were in deep trouble, and we went through a series of stages. First, we had to

HANDS-ON
LESSONS

## Managing the Transition to a No-Kidding Ownership Bonus

Often an open-book reward system will look too formidable for a company coming out of the old paradigms. To talk a full-blown No-Kidding Ownership system with short- and long-term incentives, a sense of fairness and one that truly motivates for specific value-added thinking and work is a significant chore, one that is best tackled in steps. Begin by establishing these basic practices:

- Make sure all teams and employees know what their critical numbers are and how they roll up onto the big picture financial statements.
- Make sure people earn bonuses only by adding value and understanding what they did to add value.
- Change bonus structures regularly to reflect changes in the marketplace and the company life cycle.
- Pay out bonuses frequently to generate excitement.
- Keep feedback loops short and learning-filled.
- Preach to everyone the doctrine of shared, team-based responsibility.
- Establish an atmosphere of constant learning.

Hold an offsite retreat for management to begin some of the necessary groundwork for a good incentive plan. At the retreat:

- Evaluate the effectiveness of all past programs against what you would like them to be. Use something like Figure 7–5.
- Articulate the principles you want the compensation system to adhere to, for example, "The reward system will be simple enough for all to understand, but sophisticated enough to be closely tied to short-term and long-term company goals."
- Articulate the company philosophies you want the compensation system to reinforce, for example, "The compensation plan will value and foster communication and teamwork."

| Target Employee Level | Related Objective | Type of Reward | Basis for Payout | Amount of Payout | Payout Period |
|---|---|---|---|---|---|
| Companywide | Revenue target Profit target | Bonus | $3M Revenue 20% Profit | 10% Base salary | 6 months |
| Companywide | | 401K Matching | | Up to 50% employee contribution | Year end |
| Companywide | Profitability | Profit sharing contribution | ___% of net profit | | |
| Sales consultants | Development of new business | Commission | New business | 10% | Month of closed contract |

**Figure 7–5.** Evaluation of current/past reward systems.

stop the hemorrhaging of cash. The next step was to focus on operating profit, then on net income, then on margin at the net income level. RONA was a logical next step. The target is 12.5 percent in North America, something international has already achieved. It means we're going to focus not only on the income statement, but on the effective utilization of the assets and liabilities on the balance sheet as well. I see RONA as a continuity in a progression of logical steps."

The No-Kidding Ownership RONA target is meant to create a different kind of thinking throughout the company. GM, with its many incentive plans for its many employees, expects to link more of its incentive packages to RONA as well. RONA can drive a different kind of thinking, push managers into learning more about financial measures than just profits, and even push interdepartmental teamwork with its emphasis on shared assets.

**FIELD NOTES**

## Line-by-Line Learning at Foldcraft

If a management team wants to begin practicing No-Kidding Ownership short of having a fully designed bonus plan, it could start out by offering a challenge to the employees that drives home a key financial point. For example,

Acme Products can raise profits $1 million if we sell another $13 million worth of goods. But we could also do

| Revenue | 400 |
|---|---|
| Costs of goods sold | 235 |
| Expenses | |
| • engineering | 8 |
| • insurance | 7 |
| • temporary labor | 18 |
| • travel | 12 |
| • advertising | 24 |
| • rent | 39 |
| • office | 27 |
| Profit | 30 |

This calculates to a 7.5% net profit margin.

**Figure 7–6.** Income statement for Acme Products.

it by dropping temporary labor costs from $18 million to $17 million, less than a 6 percent cut. If we do it that way we'll pay out $250,000 of that million in bonuses to celebrate our new efficiency (Figure 7–6).

This illustrates that net profits are a function of both revenues *and* expenses, that generating revenue almost always incurs additional costs, and that growing revenues is not always the best option for increasing profit. That is how a company moves a number and starts to give employees the "we-can-do-something-to-improve-financials" attitude. So ask yourself: What number on your income statement or budget could you highlight for this kind of learning?

At Foldcraft, the furniture manufacturer, business literacy really started to kick in when this kind of line-by-line impact analysis was made clear to all employees. A sample of what they call their income impact statement follows. It breaks down the line items and ties actions to the number. The following examples of Foldcraft's line-item explanations shows how specific numbers can be improved for a positive effect on the bottom line. When employees are shown *precisely* what they can do to move a number, the challenge of open-book management begins. On such knowledge is real No-Kidding Ownership based:

## From the Income Statement

*Indirect Labor:* Find ways to minimize nonproduction time in the shop, better known as improving productivity.

Each percent improvement in productivity equates to approximately $25,000 to $30,000 of profit improvement per year. Find ways to better utilize office indirect labor so that sales per office employee increases. This means that office personnel would become more efficient as business volume increases.

*Small Tools Expense and Production Supplies:* Practice better utilization of our small tools, as well as better maintenance to improve the life of these tools. Pursue suppliers that offer these products at lower prices but the same quality. This would result in having to spend less money on these items. In turn, this improves profits.

## From the Balance Sheet

*Cash and Marketable Securities:* Invest excess cash in higher yield investments so we get more interest income. Invest excess cash in tax-exempt investments because interest income is not taxable and we don't pay corporate taxes on it.

*Accounts Receivable:* Negotiate with our customers to pay earlier than 30 days and therefore we get our cash quicker and can invest it and earn interest income, adding to profit.

*Inventory: (The expected suggestions about keeping inventory low so cash is invested and not tied up.)* Designing products that use the same materials (interchangeable parts). This would allow us to carry less inventory and keep our cash invested. It also minimizes obsolete inventory, which, since it is written off, would increase profits.

**FIELD NOTES**

## The Power of Equity Incentives at SAIC

Most companies have a wide array of compensation choices: Base pay, 401Ks, and cost-of-living adjustments can be spiced with merit increases or bonuses and leavened with health coverage options, vacation policy, flextime, and child care to fashion the right blend of incentives and accountability.

One overlooked compensation lever that business literacy practices are bringing into focus is equity compensation, in which the most recent trend is stock options (Figure 7–7). While no self-respecting CEO would

|  | EMPLOYEES (MILLIONS) | PLAN ASSETS (BILLIONS) |
|---|---|---|
| ESOPS and stock bonus | 10 | $225 |
| 401Ks Mainly holding company stock | 2–3 | $200 |
| Stock options | 3 | $100 |

**Figure 7–7.** Data from the National Center for Employee Ownership.

overlook stock as part of his or her overall package, many employees will pass up the stock purchase plan because they would rather put their money in a municipal bond.

What is the difference between the CEOs and the employees? The way the company sells the stock plan and the way the employees see their role. CEOs know that if they drive the stock price up, that wealth is theirs. Employees, especially in large companies, feel that stock price is beyond their control, and that the salary is more important than the stock. The difference between CEO and employee perception lessens significantly inside open-book companies. With OBM, more employees will understand how wealth is built.

J. Robert Beyster deserves his place in the Equity Incentives Hall of Fame for his design of the compensation strategy at Science Application International Corporation (SAIC), a $2.2 billion, 22,000 employee, research-and-defense contractor that he started in San Diego in 1969. He designed the company with equity incentives foremost in mind, and now he heads the Foundation for Enterprise Development, to spread his ideas all over the rest of the world.

Dr. Beyster's following summary of how he came to open-book thinking and how SAIC applies it makes a pithy, eloquent, and compelling case for the way business should be done. It is an OBM gem. Dr. Beyster comments on his early thoughts about equity and SAIC's highly refined multipart equity-sharing system, now almost 30 years old:

**VOICES**

"I didn't worry much over the decision to share stock with the people who came to work at SAIC back in 1969, when the company was just getting off the ground. I imagine people now regard me as either wise beyond my years or out of my mind for diluting my ownership position from 100 percent to 10 percent within the first year. For me, it was simply the right thing to do—to share ownership of the company with those who make it successful. I wanted to attract smart, entrepreneurial people to our small company; I never would have predicted that this approach would fuel our growth to $2.2 billion in revenues and 22,000 employees today."

Having persuaded himself of the rightness of No-Kidding ownership Beyster had to figure out what were the right levers to pull to make employees think about the business and have a positive impact on it:

**VOICES**

"So what are SAIC's critical numbers, and how do we reward employees who have a positive impact on them? Because we are a services company, time-sold, or what is more commonly called labor utilization, drives our business. We set targets for time-sold on contract as a percentage of our labor base, and send out reports on each division's performance biweekly to almost 1,000 employees. If our time-sold targets are not met, we face staff reduction situations, so there is great awareness of our time-sold performance among all employees.

Our time-sold performance feeds directly into our second and third critical numbers—sales and profits. Our financial performance on these goals is widely discussed at our quarterly management meetings, attended by about 500 employees across the company. They return to their offices and report on our progress to the rest of the employees. We also communicate our financial performance via a quarterly report to all shareholders (almost all employees are shareholders), our employee newsletter, reports on audio cassette, our Intranet, and presentations by representatives of our employee committee. These are just a few examples of OBM principles in action at SAIC.

In the future, we will be watching two new critical numbers—cash flow and our debt-to-total capital ratio—as acquisitions become a more important part of our growth strategy. Since the early days when I mortgaged my house to finance the company, we have been able to operate largely debt-free. Today, with a few large acquisitions on the horizon, we will need to watch our cash flow to ensure we can service the related debt and our debt-to-total capital ratio to preserve our investment grade with the banks.

Perhaps even more daunting than controlling debt and cash flow, we face the challenge of developing a plan for integrating large groups of newly acquired employees into our entrepreneurial, employee-ownership culture. About 75 percent or 22,000 employees are technical professionals on contracts, responsible for delivering quality products and services, meeting budget and schedule guidelines, and pleasing the customer, which, of course, can result in follow-on business. Every single employee contributes to our growth and profitability, and thus we've spent 27 years developing our stock programs so that all employees share in the rewards. Everyone feels the impact of their work because it directly affects our stock price and their stock value."

How does Beyster connect the employees' knowledge of and impact on the business to their personal incentive? The equity sharing system he devised for SAIC is a fully integrated masterpiece:

"Our equity sharing system is designed around a simple philosophy: Those who build the company should own it, in proportion to their contribution to our growth and success. This translates into a host of programs aimed at rewarding star performers at all levels of the corporation: a deferred compensation stock award for future leaders, prenegotiated stock option awards for achieving specific performance goals, employee stock purchases matched with stock options based on performance, and annual stock bonuses. These performance-based equity incentives are coupled with programs that give all employees an opportunity to become owners: an Employee Stock Ownership Plan (ESOP), a 401(k) plan with SAIC stock as an investment choice, and a payroll withholding plan offering a 5 percent discount on stock purchases.

While it would be dangerous to try to predict the future, we know one thing for certain about today's business environment: The best, brightest, most innovative,

**VOICES**

and entrepreneurial people want a piece of the action—many won't even consider joining a company unless they receive stock. The nonprofit Foundation for Enterprise Development (FED) helps companies understand the various approaches to sharing equity. At a recent FED conference, a senior executive of an emerging Internet company commented that the technical employees he is recruiting are "smart, savvy, have done research on the company, know the potential financial gains, and are poised to negotiate their equity stake." Fortunately, or maybe unfortunately for some, this is the type of employee we all desperately need if we are to survive.

Financial success must be the end goal for every for-profit company. When employees understand what drives financial success and have a vested interest in making it happen, then you have harnessed the energy of two incredibly powerful competitive weapons."

RESOURCE: If you are interested in exploring equity compensation at your company, call the Kauffman Foundation in Kansas City, Missouri, at 1-888-777-GROW. It's Center for Entrepreneurial Leadership has published a CD to help entrepreneurs understand all their options, including issues like potentially confusing and complex tax issues. Cost: $50.

**FIELD NOTES**

## Re-Inventing the Bonus Structure

The motivating effect of "something new" is wired into our biology. Studies done on the motivational portions of the brain, particularly the hypothalamus, show that the basic mental state of humans is a vague mixture of anxiety and desire—best described by the phrase "I want," with no object for the verb.*

Thanks to the hypothalamus apparently, the job of creating work incentives will never be an easy one! Even the best bonus plan starts to lose luster over time—becoming expected. Luckily, the design possibilities for bonuses are endless. Reviewing and renewing the bonus annually is a necessary exercise to keep employees motivated. It can also be a healthy reality

---

* M. Konner, "Human Nature and Culture: Biology and the Residue of Uniqueness," *The Boundaries of Humanity* (Ed.), J. J. Sheehan and M. Sosna (Berkeley: University of California Press, 1990). pp. 103–124.

check for the company. Are there new critical numbers to consider? Given the changing environment, can the bonus be used to drive the number in different, more beneficial ways?

On the other hand, changing the bonus structure and introducing new critical numbers can breed anxiety and instability in employees at all levels. Ongoing education about what is going on and why is critical to ensure success. Consider this example:

The vice president for compensation comes back from a best practices conference all excited about a seminar she attended on Economic Value Added (EVA). This is the newest silver-bullet indicator of corporate performance that all bonuses should be based on. Sixty days later, a newly designed compensation plan is e-mailed to your work station. As a plant manager with employees who speak four languages and have many literacy problems, you have managers who don't understand *profit* let alone EVA.

EVA is a powerful integrating financial measure that has become quite popular. But for the financially uninitiated, it can be a complex concept that may be difficult to understand, needing lots of explanation. You imagine your options, at least one of which involves telling off the VP, but decide that with a little creativity and effort, educating your workers about EVA is possible.

One innovative financial manager at a medium-size plant of a Fortune 100 company was faced with just such a situation. She took the overly ambitious and too complicated measure and taught it to her managers and colleagues, union and nonunion, anyway.

She was able to turn this situation into a win-win by getting a open-book coaching company to help and using a design team. The coaches knew how to accelerate financial learning in an enjoyable, team-oriented way and the design team—comprised of managers, supervisors, and front-line union employees—was able to formulate a workable bonus structure and help teach all the employees about the business principles behind it. The union employees, who don't always get asked for their opinion on such matters, were able to make modifications to the learning objectives. They were able to add a dose of realism about how suppliers' actions and inventory problems affected profits.

**HANDS-ON
LESSONS**

## Designing a Fair and Effective Bonus

One of the more common challenges open-book companies face is equitable distribution of bonuses. It is not uncommon, for instance, for one branch or one division to account for a disproportionate percentage of the company's profits in a given year. And it's not long before someone in that successful division asks why their bonuses are the same as, or only marginally better than, others. In reality, the poorer or average performers may be doing just as well with what they have, like a tougher market or products with thinner margins.

The balancing act for managers is to create a sense of community and common destiny while at the same time allowing those who are really making it happen to feel rewarded. Short of transferring people around to walk in the other person's shoes, the best ways to strike that balance is to tie each employee's bonus to a combination of companywide, departmental, and individual measures. (See the Schrock Cabinet Company example in the Appendix.)

Here are some of the creative strategies we've observed or helped install:

- Fifty percent of the bonus depends on a corporate balance sheet item—like GM's RONA—and 50 percent depends on an individual, branch, or division income statement item like profit before tax.
- A percentage of the bonus is tied to improved performance over last year, instead of hitting an absolute number. This could be called the "prodigal son bonus system" since it provides a way to reward those who have lagged or lapsed, but manage to better themselves.
- Top management's bonuses are tied to those of the *lowest-performing* division, encouraging a vertical, team-based approach to problem solving and diffusing the tendency to assign blame.

There are two basic approaches that can help create the needed balance:

*(continued)*

- *The threshold philosophy:* Three elements of incentive pay—corporate, team, and individual—are linked to the bonus. Each element has both a threshold and a "kicker" component. The threshold is the minimum that has to be met before the others can engage. The kicker kicks in only *after* the threshold has been met. The danger is setting the threshold too high to allow good performance on the kicker components to have any payoff, which could be very frustrating (Figure 7–8).
- *The discrete elements philosophy:* Just as it implies, bonus elements are unrelated to one another, but a composite of individual targets. For example 50 percent of the bonus could be dependent on a corporate financial goal like Return on Assets, 25 percent on a team goal like on-time delivery, and 25 percent on an individual goal, like installing a new billing system.

The discrete system can be risky because, unless it's carefully designed, it could pay bonuses when the company loses money—not a good outcome or a good message to send. The smaller the company and the less cash reserves, the more important it is to keep a threshold. But if management is reasonably sure that it won't lose money, and the emphasis is on the company

| Threshold: | 1.5 to 1 = 5% Bonus<br>Plus the bonus on superior customer service can kick in for the service team, the labor efficiency bonus for the production team, and so on. |
|---|---|
| Kicker: | 1.35 to 1 = Same as above<br>(Notice lower is better, at the kicker level, only $1.35 debt exists for every $1.00 of equity) plus an additional 2% can be added to the 5%. |
| Actual performance: | 1.7 to 1 = No bonus<br>Since threshold is not met. |
| Actual performance: | 1.45 to 1 = 5% Bonus<br>Plus other bonuses for operational excellence but no kicker. |
| Actual performance: | 1.30 to 1 = The big enchilada!!!<br>Everything kicks in, including the 2% on top of the 5%. |

**Figure 7–8.** Acme bonus on debt to equity.

*(continued)*

*(Continued)*

goal, then the team and individual performance targets can work (Figure 7–9). (See the No-Kidding Ownership Bonus Systems Appendix for more ideas on incentive pay.)

| | |
|---|---|
| 50% of pay-out driven by profitability goal of 9% | pay up to 8% of salary |
| 25% of pay-out for team efficiency rating | pay up to 4% |
| 25% of pay-out for individual customer service rating | pay up to 4% |

In a service repair team of 12 people:
- 3 were given superior ratings by customers
- 8 were above average
- 1 was average

Performance
    The team received an overall rating of sup[erior in its efficiency ratings, surpassing
        the number of calls made average by 15%.
    The company's profitability was 6.5%.

Pay-out calculations:

| | |
|---|---|
| 50% for profitability: goal not reached | Zero pay-out of possible 8% |
| 25% for team efficiency rating | full pay-out for superior team rating |
| 25% for individual rating | 3 superior employees get 4% |
| | 8 above average gets 1% |
| | 1 above average gets 0% |

**Figure 7–9.** Acme bonus plan.

A year after the initial training, the certified trainers are still using the accelerated learning design to teach employees about EVA, and other plants in the company are approaching the challenge in the same way.

**FIELD NOTES**

## A Small Service Company Bonus Plan: Top and Bottom Lines and Individual Achievement

A fast-growth health care consulting and software provider that serves the home care market had been giving out bonuses to its staff since its founding in 1990. By the time the firm got above $4 million in sales with a staff size above 20, the end of the year pay-outs had, for most employees, become an expected part of the compensation, not an earned reward for high-performance. The CEO knew it was time for open-book practices to teach the staff about incentives and where the bonus was coming from.

The company CFO studies several incentive systems, went to an open-book seminar, read the books, and came up with the plan shown in Figure 7–10. The CEO had her management team go through an open-book briefing a month before the all-employee retreat. At the retreat, three weeks before the beginning of the fiscal year, all employees did some team-building and attended an open-book seminar. The management team explained the bonus in much detail, starting with a clever multiple choice quiz about the financial history and cost structure of the firm to pull everyone into the numbers and get their feet on the ground.

Armed with its new understanding, the team strategized about the plan for the coming year, and then assigned owners to each of the items in the income statement for line-of-sight accountability. They immediately began to generate discussions about some of the more obvious ways they could affect the bottom line: "I think we could get shipping down if . . ." and "We can get a better margin on the consulting when we . . ."

A new attitude about the bonus—this time based on an understanding that it would be generated only by individual achievement and hitting the company targets—was off and running.

## Putting the Bonus at Risk: The Bonus Deferral Account at Williams Pipeline

**FIELD NOTES**

Tulsa-based Williams Pipeline, with 700 employees, had a lower return on assets and generated less cash than the oil and gas industry average. Management decided they wanted to move the numbers in the right direction by making everyone responsible for improving returns and cash flow. At the same time, they wanted to dispel the fat and happy mentality that permeated the company.

After appropriate financial education so that everyone would be aware of what they could do to increase

Employee:                Sally Doe
Base Salary:             $20,000
Bonus Pool Percent:      10%
Total Standard Bonus:    $2,000

**A)  Revenue**                                        **Bonus Pool Weight      30%**
                                                       **Standard Bonus Part A  $600**

        Factor Formula = Actual Revenue
                     Projected Revenue

        Calculation:

| If Performance is: | If Factor is: | Bonus is: |
|---|---|---|
| Unacceptable | less than 85% | Factor * 0% * Standard Bonus Part A |
| Below Threshold | 85%–100% | Factor * 85% * Standard Bonus Part A |
| Threshold | 100% | Factor * 100% * Standard Bonus Part A |
| Exceeds Threshold | over 100% | Factor * 115% * Standard Bonus Part A |

**B)  Net Profit before Bonuses**                     **Bonus Pool Weight      20%**
                                                       **Standard Bonus Part B  $400**

        Factor Formula = Actual Net Profit Before Bonuses
                     Projected Net Profit Before Bonuses

        Calculation:

| If Performance is: | If Factor is: | Bonus is: |
|---|---|---|
| Unacceptable | less than 85% | Factor * 0% * Standard Bonus Part B |
| Below Threshold | 85%–100% | Factor * 85% * Standard Bonus Part B |
| Threshold | 100% | Factor * 100% * Standard Bonus Part B |
| Exceeds Threshold | over 100% | Factor * 115% * Standard Bonus Part B |

**C)  Personal Objectives**                           **Bonus Pool Weight      50%**
                                                       **Standard Bonus Part B  $1,000**

        Calculation:

| If Performance is: | Bonus is: |
|---|---|
| Unacceptable | 0% * Standard Bonus Pact C |
| Below Threshold | 50% * Standard Bonus Part C |
| Threshold | 100% * Standard Bonus Part C |
| Exceeds Threshold | 115% * Standard Bonus Part C |

---

**Figure 7–10a.** Homecare bonus plan.

| Employee: | Sally Doe |
|---|---|
| Base Salary: | $20,000 |
| Bonus Pool Percent: | 10% |
| Total Standard Bonus: | $2,000 |

**A)  Revenue**                                                **Bonus Pool Weight**      **30%**
                                                                         **Standard Bonus Part A**   **$600**

|  | Factor Formula = Actual Revenue | $4,000,000 | 100% |
|---|---|---|---|
|  | Projected Revenue | $4,000,000 | |

Calculation:

| If Performance is: | If Factor is: | Bonus Percent: | Bonus: |
|---|---|---|---|
| Unacceptable | less than 85% | 0% | |
| Below Threshold | 85%–100% | 85% | |
| **Threshold** | **100%** | **100%** | **$600** |
| Exceeds Threshold | over 100% | 115% | |

**B)   Net Profit before Bonuses**                      **Bonus Pool Weight**      **20%**
                                                                         **Standard Bonus Part B**   **$400**

|  | Factor Formula = Actual NP | $800,000 | 100% |
|---|---|---|---|
|  | Projected NP | $800,000 | |

Calculation:

| If Performance is: | If Factor is: | Bonus Percent: | Bonus: |
|---|---|---|---|
| Unacceptable | less than 85% | 0% | |
| Below Threshold | 85%–100% | 85% | |
| **Threshold** | **100%** | **100%** | **$400** |
| Exceeds Threshold | over 100% | 115% | |

**C)   Personal Objectives**                              **Bonus Pool Weight**      **50%**
                                                                         **Standard Bonus Part C**   **$1,000**

Calculation:

| If Performance is: | Bonus Percent: | Bonus: |
|---|---|---|
| Unacceptable | 0% | |
| Needs Improvement | 50% | |
| **Meeting Expectations** | **100%** | **$1,000** |
| Exceeds Threshold | 125% | |

|  | **TOTAL BONUS:** | **$2,000** |
|---|---|---|

**Figure 7–10b.**  Meeting goals.

| Employee: | Sally Doe |
|---|---|
| Base Salary: | $20,000 |
| Bonus Pool Percent: | 10% |
| Total Standard Bonus: | $2,000 |

**A) Revenue**

**Bonus Pool Weight**     **30%**
**Standard Bonus Part A**     **$600**

Factor Formula = Actual Revenue     $6,000,000     150%
Projected Revenue     $4,000,000

Calculation:

| If Performance is: | If Factor is: | Bonus Percent: | Bonus: |
|---|---|---|---|
| Unacceptable | less than 85% | 0% | |
| Below Threshold | 85%–100% | 85% | |
| Threshold | 100% | 100% | |
| **Exceeds Threshold** | **150%** | **115%** | **$1,035** |

**B) Net Profit before Bonuses**

**Bonus Pool Weight**     **20%**
**Standard Bonus Part B**     **$400**

Factor Formula = Actual NP     $1,200,000     150%
Projected NP     $800,000

Calculation:

| If Performance is: | If Factor is: | Bonus Percent: | Bonus: |
|---|---|---|---|
| Unacceptable | less than 85% | 0% | |
| Below Threshold | 85%–100% | 85% | |
| Threshold | 100% | 100% | |
| **Exceeds Threshold** | **150%** | **115%** | **$690** |

**C) Personal Objectives**

**Bonus Pool Weight**     **50%**
**Standard Bonus Part C**     **$1,000**

Calculation:

| If Performance is: | Bonus Percent: | Bonus: |
|---|---|---|
| Unacceptable | 0% | |
| Needs Improvement | 50% | |
| Meeting Expectations | 100% | |
| **Exceptional** | **125%** | **$1,250** |

| | **TOTAL BONUS:** | **$2,975** |
|---|---|---|

**Figure 7–10c.** Exceeding expectations.

Employee:                 Sally Doe
Base Salary:              $20,000
Bonus Pool Percent:         10%
Total Standard Bonus:     $2,000

**A)  Revenue**                                    **Bonus Pool Weight**        **30%**
                                                   **Standard Bonus Part A**    **$600**

Factor Formula = Actual Revenue      $3,500,000      88%
                 Projected Revenue   $4,000,000

Calculation:

| **If Performance is:** | **If Factor is:** | **Bonus Percent:** | **Bonus:** |
|---|---|---|---|
| Unacceptable | less than 85% | 0% | |
| **Below Threshold** | **88%** | **85%** | **$446** |
| Threshold | 100% | 100% | |
| Exceeds Threshold | over 100% | 115% | |

**B)  Net Profit before Bonuses**                  **Bonus Pool Weight**        **20%**
                                                   **Standard Bonus Part B**    **$400**

Factor Formula = Actual NP       $720,000      90%
                 Projected NP    $800,000

Calculation:

| **If Performance is:** | **If Factor is:** | **Bonus Percent:** | **Bonus:** |
|---|---|---|---|
| Unacceptable | less than 85% | 0% | |
| **Below Threshold** | **90%** | **85%** | **$306** |
| Threshold | 100% | 100% | |
| Exceeds Threshold | over 100% | 115% | |

**C)  Personal Objectives**                        **Bonus Pool Weight**        **50%**
                                                   **Standard Bonus Part C**    **$1,000**

Calculation:

| **If Performance is:** | **Bonus Percent:** | **Bonus:** |
|---|---|---|
| Unacceptable | 0% | |
| **Needs Improvement** | **50%** | **$500** |
| Meeting Expectations | 100% | |
| Exceptional | 125% | |

|  | **TOTAL BONUS:** | **$1,252** |
|---|---|---|

**Figure 7–10d.**  Underperforming.

cash flow, management created a quite interesting bonus structure. The formula was:

$$\begin{array}{c}\text{Operating} \\ \text{Profit}\end{array} + \begin{array}{c}\text{Book} \\ \text{Depreciation}\end{array} - \text{Taxes} - \begin{array}{c}\text{Capital} \\ \text{Expenditures}\end{array} = \begin{array}{c}\text{Cash} \\ \text{Flow}\end{array}$$

Threshold and stretch targets were set for each year, and if the stretch target was made, 5 percent of the year's pay would be put into a "bonus deferral account." The deferral account notion is a long-term at-risk idea that keeps everyone looking at the next year. Every employee can take as much as a third of his or her bonus account out in any given year. Not a bad deal—it could grow like a savings account, get sizeable, and though the yearly totals are no more than 5 percent of salary, the sum of a few years could be well into the double figures.

What keeps people focused on the long-term prize is that if threshold targets *aren't* reached, the deferral account is *at risk,* again up to 5 percent of the salary for the year. So a bad year could wipe out a good year. No one's salary is at risk, but the deferred bonus is. But it keeps people targeted on sustained performance so that short-term decisions to make this year look good at the expense of next year won't be made. And it has the added benefit of acting as a cash cushion for the company in a bad year. To keep bad years from digging a hole out of which employees won't be able to climb, the maximum negative balance that can be kept in the deferral account is –1 percent. Says Marcus Brown, director of organizational development, at Williams:

**VOICES**

"The plan is meant to align with the primary objective that our CEO has made very clear to everyone—superior sustainable results. The plan is tied very much to the sustainable part, where all our investment and equipment or plant investment decisions are tied to the long- and short-term. We are going to be in the top quartile in our industry and we are going to stay there."

This plan is only in its second year so its impact is still undetermined, the thinking is interesting, and it's gotten people's attention.

## A New Deal at Starbucks

Much of our discussion in this chapter has centered on using incentive compensation and benefits in very direct and targeted ways to drive business-critical measures. But there is another, equally important, aspect of No-Kidding Ownership that derives less from creating clear lines of sight to demonstrably move numbers and more from a philosophy of what business should be: Creating a workplace wherein everyone has a real stake and everyone is respected and looked out for. There is, no doubt, a bottom-line payoff to this, but most embark upon it because it is simply what they want their companies to stand for.

**FIELD NOTES**

One such company builder is Howard Schultz, CEO of Starbucks. If you are a latté lover you are probably unable to pass by the one of 800 Starbucks shops (they want 2000 by 2000) without popping in for a frothy brew and almond biscotti. You are not alone. In many people's opinions, including those on Wall Street, this place knows coffee. It also knows customer service. It was also an early practitioner of No-Kidding Ownership.

Like other leaders of the companies that foreshadow a new norm of partnership with employees, CEO Howard Schultz's vision is about the ephemeral side of the human experience. Schultz grew up in Brooklyn, NY, where his father was a cabdriver and holder of other low-pay, low-benefit jobs. The younger Schultz saw the negative impact the lack of a benefits safety net had on the whole family. So, at his own company, he offered workers a different deal:

"I wanted to establish the kind of company that gave people an opportunity for equity and for comprehensive health insurance, and most importantly, gave them self-esteem in the workplace. You see we're really not a profit-driven organization. We are very profitable and have exceeded the expectations of our stockholders. But we are profitable because of the value system

**VOICES**

of our company. Starbucks has given people hope in a
way. I think that's what's missing in our communities.
There's no hope."

Starbucks gives stock options and provides health insurance to all employees, even those working 20 hours
a week. Employees, referred to as partners, pay 25 percent of the premiums for themselves and 75 percent
for their dependents.

Three managed-care plans are offered; under the
preferred care option, insurance pays for 90 percent of
outpatient care with no copayment, 90 percent of hos-
pital care with a $100 copay and drugs with a $5
copay. The dental plan, which has no deductible, pays
for 100 percent of diagnostic/preventive care, 80 percent of basic procedures and 50 percent of major
procedures.

The health plans cost an average of $2,200 per
worker in 1996 for the 14,000 partners, with two-
thirds being picked up by the company.

Starbucks' health plan not only keeps employee
turnover at microscopic levels, but it also keeps employees operating at peak effectiveness. The company's ability to generate wealth for its 26-year-old
shop managers is showing us how powerful the free
enterprise system is for capturing the human imagination when employees are aligned with shareholders.

Perhaps that's the final word on incentives. No system is fault-free and no single incentive works miracles by itself. Don't overemphasize the bonus or any
other kind of incentive. Have a philosophy of fun, fairness, recognition, respect, celebrations, learning, and
achievement. If you accomplish that, employees will
consider the bonus icing and not the cake.

# 8

## *Player-Coach Leadership*

### Learning Executive Skills for an Open-Book World

*Once the company got to a certain size I wasn't being treated as one of the team anymore. I was the CEE—EE—OH, and pretty much, people wouldn't challenge my decisions. So I created a manager triad—an operations person, a salesperson, and one from corporate—and, as a group, they could overrule me. It made it easier for them. It worked so great that after they got used to overruling me, they started doing it individually. So we didn't need the triads anymore—they're gone. They overrule me all the time now. They're making decisions—and I'm back on the team.*

Patrick Kelly
CEO
Physician Sales and Service

Tampa-based Physician Sales and Service (PSS), with $700 million in sales, 69 branches, rapid growth, and big plans for the future cultivates its leaders with skill-building exercises in listening, giving feedback, problem solving, and reading Plato.

Plato? "You can learn a lot as a leader from the questions he raises," says CEO Patrick Kelly, a charismatic leader who thinks of his business in a larger social context—just the kind of thing reading Plato stimulates.

Kelly deeply believes in the power of leadership, the limits of power, and that open-book companies foster widespread responsibility: "We want our managers to know that they work for their people and not the other way around." Kelly believes this is especially true for the CEO, as evidenced by his opening comments.

This kind of thinking is at the core of Player-Coach Leadership, where all the coaches, even the CEO, stay close to the action and the front-line. And, conversely, all the players, by virtue of the fact that they have responsibility, exercise leadership and make decisions. At the senior-manager levels, the shift in thinking and behavior from the days of top-down thinking to open-book management requires Patrick Kelly-type judgments on how an enterprise should govern itself.

Player-Coach Leadership is rooted in questions of human governance, the kind Plato pursued. It confers on *every* employee the responsibility to meet business challenges. And it requires recognition of the fact that, while some are natural leaders in certain settings, we all lead and take care of ourselves.

Our first book spent the better part of two chapters on leadership skills and requirements in open-book settings. We were trying to send a message—open-book practices, the observable set of behaviors and systems that create a company of businesspeople focused on results, all start with leadership.

Jean Paul Sartre was asked near the end of his life how he would have done things differently if given a second chance. He responded, "I would have been more radical." More than a year after publishing our first book, that's exactly how we feel about the absolute necessity for quality leadership in an open-book environment. Had we known then what we know now, we would have been even more radical in our stance: *The right kind of leadership is absolutely critical to open-book success.*

Whole Foods Market CEO John Mackey makes it very clear that the entire structure of his business, highly decentralized and totally teamed, is designed to promote responsible, high-thinking leadership skill. He has been building the now 10,000 employee, Austin, Texas-based company since 1982—open-book and open-salary since 1987—on the principles of Player-Coach Leadership wherein everyone exercises authority on a level playing field. If Patrick Kelly put a limit on CEO power, Mackey says he has "put a limit on management greed." The highest paid personnel get no more than eight times the average pay of all employees.

The essence of the $1 billion natural foods grocer is providing a service in the marketplace that enriches the customer's body and soul, and offering it in such a way that the service providers, the employees, are enabled and ennobled by the work:

"We try to organize our work in such a way that all the needs of our employees are satisfied. We use human potential psychologist Abraham Maslow's hierarchy of human needs as a guide to see how we are doing. Employees are always going to complain, but we want them complaining about the right thing—not "will I get my next paycheck" (the need for security, the lowest level on the hierarchy), but "I hope I get to switch to another team soon so I can pursue that kind of work (the need for growth, the highest level)."

**Voices**

Whole Foods Market pursues social goals as part and parcel of the enterprise, goals that resonate in the heart, not just the heads and the pocketbooks, of employees:

"We want to stop the degradation of food that has become commonplace in the food industry the last 60 years. We want to help our customers transform their diets and live healthier lives, and we want to support sustainable agriculture."

**Voices**

Missions like that turn open-book management into the force it can become, a set of practices built on a belief system that releases all the energies employees can bring to work—mind, heart, and hands. Missions—and companies—like that are the direct product of real leadership. To provide that kind of leadership, you must cultivate the following skills:

1. Master the basics of the business.

2. Make your learning process—and mistakes—a visible example.

3. Tell stories that convey meaning.

4. Create other open-book leaders.

5. Embrace the people-and-profits paradox.

6. Stay both part of the team and in charge.

7. Lead and manage simultaneously.

8. Create community in *and beyond* your company.

9. Blend intuition and numbers know-how.

10. Create miracles by looking for them.

Not all leaders in business-literate companies have the same mix of these skills. With the usual bent for variety, open-book managers get the job done in their own way and style. But as a standard to follow, these skills are worth developing across the company. In the remainder of this chapter, we will elaborate on the need for each of these skills and illustrate how they play out in day-to-day and long-term management.

## SKILL 1: MASTER THE BASICS OF THE BUSINESS

In open-book environments, managers and team leaders are responsible for transferring knowledge. This first requires that the managers themselves know the business fundamentals. Then the transference of knowledge and insight does not take place overnight, or at one meeting. It is an ongoing process of discussion and querying, probing and testing until, hopefully, employees surpass their managers in knowledge and skill and achieve new levels of competence and performance. It is not a linear process, but a cyclical one, and the leader's work is never complete.

Institute the practice at Huddles, of having employees tackle a business problem that management sees, and do it when possible in terms of dollars and cents. It could be a customer problem, a supplier problem, a turnover problem, but let employees chew on the issues and create possible solutions.

At select times, most likely when the problems and challenges come into focus, have employees, not management, create a business case for a new product, capital purchase, or new delivery process. Put the employees in cross-functional teams and have them analyze the issue, present the solutions on a one-page summary document, and see what they come up with. Jerome A. Harris, Managing Partner at American Express Tax & Business Services, comments on the need for constant reinforcement of OBM thinking:

Voices

"In order to be an effective leader, you must take every conceivable chance to have a dialogue on your business' critical numbers. It is only through this repetition that your employees will understand their financial impact. At one time, I believed that all I had to do was tell my partners *once* what they had to accomplish and how to measure their individual accomplishments. I have finally learned that this does not keep them focused. What they constantly need is reinforcement of what is expected. I finally came to realize what advertising professionals have known from the start. You get your message across by repeating it as many times as possible. This, over time, will lead to acceptance and understanding. Your job as a leader is to make sure that there are no excuses for not understanding the numbers."

## SKILL 2: MAKE YOUR LEARNING PROCESS—AND MISTAKES— A VISIBLE MODEL

Open books make problems visible. Variances against a plan pop up all the time, and when a team doesn't meet its number, the team has to start questioning why: Was the plan ambitious, was it stupid? Did a process get out of control? How can we get it under control? What do we have to learn to do better next month, quarter, year? If we add this feature to the service, will it be worth the additional revenue?

Player-coach leaders are in the habit of asking questions for themselves and the team without having all the answers. They show their learning process to others, demonstrating the value of team thinking, making mistakes, and soliciting feedback about their skills.

The best way to create an environment where employees can admit, not hide, their mistakes, and then share the learning, is to have leaders regularly admit what they learned through the mistakes they made. Practice phrases like, "Here's where I went wrong" and "I didn't realize this when I made that decision" and "That was my best judgment, but what I didn't take into consideration was . . ." The example of the boss is crucial here—people need permission to learn from mistakes and openly speak about them.

Take the idea of learning seriously and institutionalize the learning goals as part of the human resource/ performance management system. Bob Argabright, formerly of Chesapeake Packaging, is an excellent example of this:

**VOICES**

"Each individual needs to view himself as the "president" of his own individual company. If the numbers cannot be managed at the individual level, it is impossible to manage them from the organizational level. At

Chesapeake, each employee was in our performance management system. They were assigned a coach, and we eliminated the top-down aspect, replacing it with a personalized bottom-up review system."

Argabright sees this as the key to the open-book approach, "No one escapes personal accountability." Figure 8–1 is part of the 90-day review form Chesapeake used.

*My Action Plan for Helping Us Be the Best in Employee Performance*

| **What** I will do is _____ | **Action #** |
|---|---|
| _____ . | |

**When?** _____ .

**How?** _____

_____ .

**Who else** will participate? _____ .

**How I** will **measure** this action is _____

_____ .

**Follow-up #1** _____

_____ .

**Follow-up #2** _____

_____ .

**Date completed** _____

**The results were** _____

_____

_____ .

**Figure 8–1.** Employee performance.

# SKILL 3: TELL STORIES THAT CONVEY MEANING

*Not everything that can be counted counts and not everything that counts can be counted.*

Anonymous

Open-book environments are numbers-obsessed. But player-coach leaders aren't number crunchers with the personalities of calculators. The stories behind the numbers make the difference and convey the meaning of and purpose for the numbers in the first place.

When a customer service representative asks why revenue went up 10 percent this month, a natural time for storytelling occurs. Instead of explanations like "We sold more of the Acme deluxe product," or "We introduced the new product," the player-coach leader has a great opportunity to animate the number, paint a three-dimensional picture, and reinforce *everyone's* role in the success:

**VOICES**

"Remember all the work in product development last year on the Acme deluxe? We even made some customer response calls out of here. Well, the product is looking good. Not only does the second month impact take our sales up, we've got more requests for next quarter than we can handle. The product development team is revved. Bill put so much time in on this introduction in front of the customers, they're calling him "the sales master" now."

People can argue with data. They have a hard time arguing with stories. One reason stories are powerful is that they appeal to the imagination. Unlike data, which appeals to the fact-based side of our thinking processes, stories create pictures and sounds in our heads. Stories teach what is valuable and convey meaning in ways that facts can't. And they create a context that makes the facts all the more powerful.

Not all managers are born storytellers. But with practice and a model to follow and encouragement from upper management, middle managers and supervisors can start embellishing the examples that create an open-book culture.

Managers at open-book exemplar MANCO use stories regularly to convey the energy and commitment of their culture. Listen to Cheryl Dimattia from MANCO's human resources department:

> "At MANCO, everybody's experience and learning is valued, so it doesn't take you too long to get the idea that you can share your experience in the form of a story. It all starts with CEO Jack Kahl, who is constantly sharing information with clear examples—and the examples become stories. It takes maybe 6 months for employees to get what this storytelling in meetings is all about. It's one of the major ways we transfer what we are learning—it's how we celebrate—it's how we have fun."

**VOICES**

And stories convey the values of customer service and efficiency and creativity and everything else that humans care about. Stories make the numbers sing. As Stanley Crawford in *A Garlic Testament—Seasons on a Small New Mexico Farm* said:

> "The financial statement must finally give way to the narrative, with all its exceptions, special cases, imponderables. It must finally give way to the story, which is perhaps the way we arm ourselves against the next and always unpredictable turn of the cycle in the quixotic dare that is life . . . (the story) is our seed, our clove, our filament cast toward the future."

**VOICES**

## SKILL 4: CREATE OTHER OPEN-BOOK LEADERS

The ultimate act of leadership is to create more leaders. Open-book management creates a yeasty learning environment where people can push their learning in both job and business skills. Web Converting's Rob Zicaro explains why it is critical that player-coach leaders work to help their teams grow:

**VOICES**

"Cultivating a competitive advantage demands leadership throughout an organization, not just from the top. It's vital that leaders emerge in all areas of the company, particularly on the front lines where the work is performed. Machine operators need to be champions of business literacy as well as front-line administrators and support people. A compelling, passionate presence of leaders in the midst of the culture solidifies open-book management as a permanent force, not a passing fad."

Management has been defined as using people to get work done. Player-coach leaders know that leadership is using work to hone people. Some managers never get promoted because they never create their own replacements. In open-book companies, teaching someone to do your job so you can move on *is* the goal. A formal way to start making this happen is to use the Huddle process. A good Huddle System has a healthy amount of status and peer pressure attached to it— can you deliver on the numbers that your team committed to in the plan? Having teammates attend the Huddles with their managers to get a first hand feel for the process, and then having them attend on their own, is a great train-your-replacement tool.

Many open-book companies develop their leaders by moving employees around in the organization so they can get a dose of reality while learning from all perspectives. Chris Rooney brought open-book to the government systems division of Sprint Business when he was its president. He introduced an effective executive rotation program that came to be known as the *executive swirl program* because of the intense learning demands it placed on participants. One of Rooney's managers commented that she could feel herself "circling the drain." Amusing, but it also makes a point.

Open-book practices can make people uncomfortable—learning and stretching can often have that effect. It is the job of the leader to commiserate, coach, coax, cajole, and demand all at the same time.

## SKILL 5: EMBRACE THE PEOPLE-AND-PROFITS PARADOX

Business has long operated under the following assumption: Numbers are hard and nitty-gritty; people issues are soft and touchy-feely. Not true. Player-coach leaders know the company culture dictates whether numbers are met and use that to teach, develop, coach, and motivate.

Player-coach leaders must be the mechanism by which soul is put in the numbers and the numbers are put in people's souls. Most companies have the explicit goal of giving a good return to its shareholders. It can be no different for employees if open-book management is to mean anything. Create a mission statement that *all* stakeholders, including customers, shareholders, and employees can call their own. One company put it this way:

> "We will provide a better-than-average return to our shareholders, attracting more capital for our ongoing growth. We will pay our employees above the prevailing market salaries by achieving our incentive pay goals. In this way, we will attract the most talented people, create a loyal workforce, and make it possible for all employees to improve the quality of their lives."

**VOICES**

Having a mission is one thing, but persuading employees that there is a direct link between their performance and their standard of living is another. It won't be easy. In a 1996 study conducted by Watson Wyatt Worldwide, a compensation firm, only 28 percent of employees surveyed saw a connection between their performance and their pay. Backing up your mission

with your tactics and your words—that is, *leadership*—
will make the difference.

## SKILL 6: STAY BOTH A PART OF THE TEAM *AND* IN CHARGE

Followers want their leaders to be a cut above them—
sometimes. Followers also want their leaders to look
and be competent, to command respect, represent
them well, teach the business, and excel in the numbers. To do this, leaders need to accept the status that
comes with their competence or position, and look
and act the part.

But player-coaches are also players. They roll up
their sleeves and get their hands dirty. They ask questions about the numbers, show their limitations, get
advice, and follow it as part of the team they coach.
When necessary, they can ignore their status and become part of the group.

This capacity to be both very human and a cut
above is difficult for those managers who are afraid to
be visible and take charge, and just as hard for those
leaders who have spent their professional lives learning how to use status and its symbols.

As a leader, it is okay, indeed desirable, to make
yourself approachable, accessible, and *human.* A little
self-deprecation goes a long way—and it costs you
nothing. We've seen some of the most accomplished
open-book leaders poke fun at themselves in holiday
skits, give out awards to employees who do the best
imitation of their management foibles, and *knowing*
they are terrible at softball, allow themselves to get
thoroughly whupped at the company softball game.

Now and then, a wry little comment like, "I had a
new idea about that problem . . . which now gives me
two for this decade," buy more credibility and good-
will than all the business smarts you can muster. This

takes a little bit of effort and practice, and it can be overdone; but in small doses, and if genuine, it builds tremendous *esprit de corps.* It is a balancing act, to be sure, but making yourself credible in both the roles of coach *and* player is a valuable leadership skill critical to the success of open-book management.

To complement this effort, you also want to help your employees to be credible not only as players, but also as *coaches.* The simple way of sending this message is to give teams the work, responsibility, and authority formerly reserved for managers—to essentially redefine the notion of middle management to mean not individuals, but self-directed *teams* of employees. For all the talk about self-directed work teams the last decade, much more needs to be done. The Association for Quality and Participation conducted a 1995 study reporting that only 15 percent of the participation processes attempted have made any substantial change in the way business is done. Employees, even if on teams, are still on the outside looking in because managers make most of the decisions.

Don't miss the opportunity to create real functional teams. OBM confers on employees the kind of knowledge, responsibility, and motivation it takes to allow a front-line team to be *truly* self-directed and make smart decisions. To promote business literacy without shifting workloads and decision-making authority to teams is a waste of energy. Again, the difference between failure and success is the catalyst that leadership provides. Listen to the words of Syncrude CFO Phil Lachambre:

"As departmental redesign projects have been implemented over the past few years, middle management has had to work to understand the meaning of management and leadership in a new form of work organization. Some significant progress has been made with notions about team management structures. Part of this work has involved defining the relationship between semi-autonomous work teams and middle management.

VOICES

We've found that the new form of work organization controls variances *at source* more rigorously than traditional organizations."

## SKILL 7: LEAD AND MANAGE SIMULTANEOUSLY

You see it a lot. The people who lead organizations can often inspire and create change, but also excel at creating chaos. They couldn't manage the local Dairy Queen. In other words, natural leadership tendencies and strong management skills are often not linked traits. And organizations suffer from the disconnection between leadership (vision and strategy) and management (execution and administration).

With OBM, the tension between leadership and management becomes less an issue. Those with natural leadership tendencies will be able to keep the house in order because open-book management relies on a plan, Huddles and feedback, data and variances, the traditional tools of managers. Those with natural gifts for management and control will have to share information, empower their teams to plan, teach, motivate with recognition and bonuses, and animate the numbers with stories and meaning. These are the usual tools of leadership. Leadership is not good and management bad, or vice versa. Player-coach leaders will combine and use both skills and all the tools in open-book systems.

Bob Argabright's account of his journey into open-book management is all about the best of both management and leadership:

VOICES

"In looking back over my past thirty years with Chesapeake Corporation, it is difficult to identify my first experience with open-book management. My assignments from 1972 to 1981 were in the role of a "turnaround" specialist and from 1981 to 1988 as a corporate officer with the company. In 1988, I assumed the position of president and general manager of the Chesapeake-Baltimore facility, which was in financial difficulty. The Corporation had also stated that "people are our most valuable resource"—something I had always believed—but it never demonstrated in any way that this was true. I wanted to make this a reality. I found a way to establish instant credibility: to share the numbers and to focus on a 1 percent improvement in all areas that our people could control. My view had always been to lay out all the facts about a situation and ask for people's personal commitment to make a difference. I thought people as well as the business could excel in this type of organizational climate. The approach worked better than I had ever dreamed it could."

## SKILL 8: CREATE COMMUNITY WITHIN AND BEYOND YOUR COMPANY

Open-book techniques are useful to the degree that they create purpose-filled, learning-driven, goal-committed companies. Individual accomplishment is valued by player-coach leaders but group accomplishment is valued more. From the bonus systems in No-Kidding Ownership to the inclusiveness of Huddles and financial know-how, the *power of the team and company as a whole* is emphasized.

Common destiny is a hallmark of open-book companies, instead of the us-versus-them thinking that kills long-term superior performance. As much as the systems of open-book companies stimulate the continued growth of intelligent organizations, they also promote the possibility of adult learning communities, bonded by trust and driven by the hope of moving closer to their visions. They are good for the heart and head as well as the bottom line.

In our stress-filled world, researchers have discovered that a life without heart, without caring or passion or trust or fun, is a life heading for burnout and despair. One such researcher, James J. Lynch, has written extensively about the ills that befall individuals and companies that ignore the need for community:

> So vital to human health is the language of our hearts that—if ignored, unheard, or misunderstood—it can produce terrible physical suffering, even premature death. For the language of our hearts cries out to be heard. It demands to be understood. And it must not be denied. Our hearts speak with an eloquence that poets always and truly sensed. It is for us to learn to listen and to understand.*

Player-coach leaders understand the language of the human heart at work. They understand that while employees are at work, mustering their competitive juices to create wins in the marketplace, they need a community of common destiny to be a part of where trust outweighs conflict and doing good makes the hard effort pay off.

Between 1990 and 1994, when we were partners with Springfield Remanufacturing where much of the seminal work defining OBM was done, CEO Jack Stack made a telling comment about the metrics of a successful open-book company:

**VOICES**

"One thing we look for to know if we are doing the right thing as a company is to see how many of our employees are volunteering for activities in the community. If they are, in good numbers, then we know they are feeling good enough about their lives, their careers, and their company that they can afford to give something back to the community."

Not a bad metric for a numbers-obsessed, premier, open-book company! How many volunteers in the community are there from your company? Could your team support Junior Achievement, promote United

---

* James J. Lynch, *The Language of the Heart*, New York: Basic Books, 1985, p. 10.

Way, adopt a school, or find some other rallying point for values-based team effort beyond the immediate needs of the company?

At Foldcraft, the idea of creating community, the notion that the whole is bigger and more important than the parts, became clear in a quite unexpected way. During a traumatic downsizing, the very kind of event that normally fractures community rather than builds it, the powerful results of open-book philosophy were dramatically demonstrated to CEO Steve Sheppard:

**VOICES**

"Our assumptions about the power of this process were perhaps best and most unexpectedly affirmed during the most difficult episode of the company's past 20 years. Perhaps partially as a result of our open-book awakening, a stem-to-stern assessment of how we conducted our business was undertaken. It was performed by a committee cross-section of the organization, and it led to the inescapable conclusion that staffing levels were too high in relation to how we need to conduct our business competitively. After great brainstorming sessions about other ways in which some of these people could be used, the committee still arrived at the need for reduction in the workforce. This is action that is miserable enough for any organization, but even more wrenching within an organization that is employee-owned.

Despite the personal sensitivity that everyone brought to this trauma, despite the provision of grief and outplacement counseling, despite the severance arrangements created just for this occasion, it was a miserable, rotten affair. Some of the departing members had been friends and associates for a long time. The entire day was a teary one. And despite what I imagined would be deep resentment toward anyone from the management ranks by those leaving the organization, I felt the need to say goodbye on that morning, to say thanks and Godspeed to some good people.

The affirmation of our teaching occurred in the moments just before, during, and within 10 days following the event. During that period, no fewer than eight of those individuals, all of whom had been uprooted from their work and daily routines, approached me personally or telephoned me to say basically the following:

I know why the company felt the need to do this. I understand what changes the company will realize from this. I think it may be good for the company. (And in one case) I don't know why it took you so long. I'm just sorry that I had to be one of the ones affected by it. I wish I could be here for the changes.

I'm not sure what I expected to hear from people faced with this trauma in their lives, but it definitely was not this! And it was only after some reflection that I came to realize that what I was hearing was the understanding of what makes a business work, of the realities of financial vitality and competitiveness and agility. I was listening to those eight people recite part of what had been learned in those hours of open-book education. The individuals were not happy, to be sure. But they had an appreciation of what was behind the change sufficient to defuse the personal effrontery that is normally such a big part of these circumstances. I felt reasonably certain that these eight people, at least, would have no difficulty in finding employment elsewhere because they possessed a perspective that is valued in companies: that of a businessperson. (Each of the eight was, in fact, hired shortly after their departure from Foldcraft, to the great gain of those new employers!) Open-book management cannot guarantee employment, but it can better assure employability.

What allowed this level of maturity and understanding to occur? I have to believe that it flowed from the variety and frequency of open-book efforts which the company has adopted over the years."

## SKILL 9: BLEND INTUITION AND NUMBERS KNOW-HOW

In baseball, statistics and physics indicate that left-handed batters have a harder time hitting balls thrown by left-handed pitchers. Good managers play the percentages a lot: When a dangerous lefty comes to the plate, the skipper will call to the bullpen to counter with a southpaw—almost always the way to go. But occasionally you see somebody play a hunch and go to the bullpen for the right-hander. And sometimes, wonderfully, it works.

Fact-based, financially sound decisions drive open-book management. But, as in sports and most other endeavors, intuition picks up where the numbers leave off. Spreading information and facts around the company allows entire workforces to manage variances. It helps coordinate efforts and keeps outside business conditions and inside work processes continually connected. But all the facts in the world won't eliminate business risks. And changes in customers and environments mean making decisions for which the numbers have yet to indicate a trend. In such cases, sometimes you'll have to call in the right-hander.

Knowing when not to use the numbers, when to flip between decision-making modes, when to get facts and when to explore assumptions, is player-coach leadership at work. The human mind and heart know more than the mouth can explain and give voice to. At times logic chains are clear; if A then B, if B then C, and so on. Other times the mind jumps from A to Q, and it's a good decision.

That is why the Huddle, with its forecasting element, acts as a cornerstone of open-book management. It teaches the reality of being accountable without having all the facts. The Huddle teaches the essence of analytical and intuitional thinking. As soon as an employee has a number for which she is responsible, an understanding of why the number is important and of the factors that affect it, she can forecast. The less information, the more intuition needs to be used. Both logic and intuition are valuable processes because both—and most people do not realize this—are based on knowledge. They are both tools available only to those who are informed, not only by facts, but also by processes, tendencies, behaviors, and underlying principles.

One of the best ways to stimulate this kind of bimodal thinking is through game-playing and role-playing. In any game—just as in business—you are employing skills, using intuition, and, to some degree, counting on luck to create a favorable outcome. In our *Profit and Cash* game, participants use skill in assessing risks and deciding how big a loan should be, for instance, while a roll of the dice may determine the volume of the sale. If you use a game to teach this element of leadership, make sure to debrief the game with a big emphasis on this question: "When did we use logic in this process and when did we go with our intuition."

Pat Kelly at Physician Sales and Service designed their Huddle, called the PSS Challenge, to quiz and reward his employees around the numbers that matter, encouraging the use of both logic and intuition. The best open-book leaders create fun and learning in their companies all the time by setting up this kind of thinking.

## SKILL 10: CREATE MIRACLES BY LOOKING FOR THEM

Player-coach leaders look beyond the routine elements of work to what is marvelous, even miraculous in what goes on every day. Maslow, the father of human potential thinking, commented on every day and its possibilities: "The people who look for miracles have it all wrong. When you look at something right, everything is miraculous."

Player-coach leaders create the little surprises that maintain peak interest; whether it's a refreshing way to recognize an accomplishment, a new insight into a customer, or a nephew's story about school and what it has to say about people and the way we learn.

Player-coach leaders see the latent miracles in the routine stuff of work. Financial reports and budgets become a series of promises between teams. Staff meetings become opportunities for learning and dialogue, commitments and covenants, celebration and growth. Normally just a way to make a living, work it-self is also a way to connect to living, breathing, all-important customers, to create a livelihood, and to change the planet with purpose and ennobling effort.

As a player-coach leader, if you are going to teach your employees and teammates anything about the enduring value of building a business and serving customers, you need to cultivate this soulful capacity in yourself. When the phone won't quit, meetings are near wall-to-wall, and conflicts and undone work abound, go outside and walk around the building and look for some growing thing, like a dandelion, or a cloud formation that tickles your fancy, or a car in the parking lot that is beautifully designed. See the under-lying, latent power and beauty in the everyday stuff of all life, including business life. Then communicate it.

Seeing all these miracles requires an attitude—and successful player-coaches like Foldcraft's Steve Shep-pard have it:

> "I like to think of leadership within the company in holistic terms, with dimensions that are intellectual, so-cial, emotional, spiritual, occupational, and physical. The company, like each of the individuals in it, requires attention to each of these elements if it's going to maximize its potential."

**VOICES**

Foldcraft does a number of things exceedingly well as an open-book company. One of the features that sets it apart from many is the commitment it has to the full development of its people, including their spiritual sides.

A program Foldcraft offers its employees (members) is called "Cross-Boundaries." Sheppard describes:

> "Foldcraft Co. aggressively embraced the concepts of true entrepreneurial ownership, open-book manage-ment, and the full human development of each of its 300 members, by both traditional and nontraditional means. "Cross-Boundaries" is an opportunity for Fold-craft's members to travel to other parts of the world

**VOICES**

for the purpose of experiencing life in a far different context. The trips are normally to Third World countries where poverty and oppression are constant. Such travel can be life changing.

Foldcraft Co. regards these learning opportunities as important pieces of a holistic development process of our member-owner. It broadens thinking and awareness of how others live, what we have, what our obligations are in our own lives and elsewhere in the world. And it educates our members about the incredible diversities that exist in the world. As we discover the value of such differences, we become more accepting of what each human being has to offer to the collective effort, both in the company and the world at large. This discovery helps to affirm the sanctity and value of every human life. Finally, "Cross-Boundaries" gives members a global and cultural sensitivity. As we expand into foreign markets, this appreciation becomes critical to both our corporate social responsibility and our ability to adapt to such markets. Understanding global markets requires an appreciation of the people and cultures creating them, and what impact our presence on those people and cultures may be.

The trips are usually one or two weeks long. Foldcraft provides the paid time to the participant, while the expenses of the trips are covered by donors to the various nonprofit organizations that arrange these trips, such as the Center of Global Education or Habitat for Humanity. The only requirement of a participant is that he or she share the feelings experienced from the trip with fellow members upon return. Any member of Foldcraft who has completed one year of employment is eligible for "Cross-Boundaries," without loss of compensation or use of vacation time. Further, participants become eligible for a second such experience after a 3-year period.

We view "Cross-Boundaries" as wellness education that broadens the character, business perspectives, and sense of humanity in our members."

Dawn Rohl, an 11-year Foldcraft member who runs its computers, experienced such a life change when she went to El Salvador for 10 days in 1994:

"I'll never forget seeing what those people go through. And they survive, keep smiling, keep moving ahead with faith. It made me more upbeat, more positive."

**VOICES**

Chip Krueger, a Foldcraft member who manages the lumber yard and operates a kiln, went to southern Mexico in late 1996 to build homes in two villages eight hours from Mexico City:

"It was so eye-opening. It made me look hard at what I think is important. I'd go back in a minute. The people there didn't know where the United States was. I remember most the smiling cute kids in the villages . . . and all the people living on the landfill we drove by. Foldcraft gives us the chance to experience this. I'd recommend it to anyone."

**Voices**

Player-coach leaders weave their dreams so that others can have the opportunity to weave theirs. The managers at Web Industries have allowed machinists like Rob Zicaro to weave some of his own, and to comment on what the miracle of work means to him:

"As we move along this life-long learning experience, we must remember that the numbers are reflections of what is or is not happening in our business cultures. It's as if we're holding up a mirror and a virtual image of our organization is reflected back at us. In many cases, it's the "intangible assets" that are undeveloped and malnourished. Trust, caring, respect, passion, love, creativity, and interpersonal relationships all play a determining role in a company's financial success and growth. I know they don't show up in black and white on the income statement, however these attributes within our people make up the foundation of our human capital, the most precious asset in any organization."

**Voices**

# Epilogue

Open-book management is a major refinement of the capitalistic system. As Max Depree, former chairman of Herman Miller says: "The capitalist system has excluded too many people from both the process and generally equitable distribution of results . . . most people never get the opportunity to be meaningfully involved."

The following encounter, as brief as a taxicab ride, describes how important the free enterprise system is for people across the world. And it should remind us of why opening the books is important—involving more of us preserves and improves the system we can too easily take for granted.

One of the more poignant cabbie stories we've heard was from a Moroccan driver who drove us to a hotel in Indianapolis for a seminar with the CEOs of The Executive Committee. He matter-of-factly recounted how he was educated in France, had spent six years practicing his profession, had two kids that were the center of his and his wife's lives, and whom he hadn't seen in the two years he had been driving a cab.

This gentleman had escaped the political repression in Morocco, which began in earnest in the 1980s. When things got serious, this man fled to the United States to pursue his dream of freedom and to study and find work in his old profession. When he wasn't working, he was preparing to pass the required exam.

"I think I can get my family here in a year or two," he said. "But if I can't pass the exams, I will have to look for work that will sustain us somehow." He was one story among thousands, people trying to come to the land of the free and the land of business opportunity. He cherished and fought to participate in a system that many of us take for granted.

"I never thought I'd be driving a cab for a living," he said with some obvious strain in his voice. "But while I do have to do it, I may as well try to do a good job of it."

The exam he was studying for was a medical board. In Morocco, this man had been a practicing physician. The cab driver was a doctor trying to re-establish himself and his family.

Free enterprise is a system that business literacy and open-books must preserve and enhance for ourselves and for displaced free souls that need a second chance.

# *Appendix I*

## No-Kidding Ownership
## Bonus Examples

The following are actual examples of companies implementing open-book incentive pay systems. We chose them—one service and one manufacturing—because they are typical, not brilliant or extraordinary. The first one, LTQ, while real, has a fictional name. The second one is real and actual: Schrock Cabinet Company. We've included the written communication, not the only one, that accompanied the announcement of the bonus.

These bonus examples work best when tied to specific line-of-sight and Huddle practices. They provide the framework for improving performance, but the score carding at the team and front-line level will determine if all employees view the bonus plan as real to them.

# Example 1

MEMORANDUM

To:      All Associates
From:   Harriet, CFO
Re:      LTQ Goal '97
Date:    April 17, 1997

As we continue our process of defining Open-Book Management for LTQ, we are excited to present our goals for this fiscal year. We are almost half way through our fiscal year and therefore have a very short time to reach our target.

We have decided on two goals for LTQ Goal 97: a revenue goal and a net profit goal. It is possible to make either goal, neither, or both.

To simplify the drive toward Goal 97, we have decided upon a minimum cash balance goal. Our minimum cash balance must be $350,000 at year end, in addition to the bonuses, profit sharing, and 401K matching payable at the end of the year. This minimum cash balance is very important in order to ensure that we have cash available to pay the bonuses and to run the company in the following quarter. It assures us that our revenue is not tied up in "old" receivables or spent for capital assets.

In addition to the minimum cash balance, we are also setting a minimum profit level of $300,000 at year-end. Our net profit goal is set at a minimum dollar amount of $300,000 to cover the situation in which we could have very low revenues but still be very profitable at the same time. The $300,000 is needed to fund the continuing operations of LTQ for our next fiscal year and to ensure the security of all our jobs. If we were to reach our minimum revenue goal of $2.5 million and a profit level of 16%, we would have profits of $400,000. You can see that the $300,000 profit level should be obtainable if we achieve our anticipated revenue level and profit percentage.

*(continued)*

Because both cash flow and profitability are equally important, payment of bonuses at the percentages outlined here can't be guaranteed if we do not achieve both the minimum $350,000 cash balance and the $300,000 profit minimum.

The revenue and profit goals are weighted so that most of the financial benefit (85%) is paid if our net profit goal is achieved. We did this because it's possible to have very large revenue numbers without having profitable projects. If this were the case, we wouldn't have any dollars available to pay the bonuses. Our incremental revenue goals for Goal 97 will be $2.5 million, $3.0 million, and $3.5 million as discussed at our annual meeting and again at our introduction to Open-Book Management meeting. If our annual revenue is less than $2.5M, no revenue bonuses are guaranteed.

The three net profit payout levels will be at 16 percent of revenue, 17.4 percent of revenue, and 20 percent of revenue. Net profit is defined as profit before taxes, profit-sharing contribution, 401K matching contributions, and bonuses. Last year our net profit was just over 17 percent and in 1993 it was over 31 percent. You can see that our payout levels are obtainable! If our net profit level is less than 16 percent of revenue, no profit bonuses will be guaranteed. We will pay a profit bonus at a revenue minimum of $2.0M.

The structure of Goal 97 will give each of us the opportunity to receive bonuses of up to 24 percent of our individual salaries. When you add to this the anticipated profit sharing and 401K matching contributions, this number jumps to 32.5 percent of salary. Grab a calculator and multiply your annual base salary by these percentages. I think the numbers will WOW you!

If we make our minimum revenue goal of $2.5 million and our minimum profit goal of 16 percent, the bonus percentage will be 10 percent of salaries of 18.19 percent, including estimated profit sharing and 401K matching. There are schedules attached that lay out some of the different possibilities and percentages.

For example: An LTQ employee earning $20,000 a year, would get a bonus (before profit sharing and 401K matching) like this:

*(continued)*

| Revenue | LTQ Net Profit % | % of Salary | Dollars |
|---|---|---|---|
| $2.5 Million | 16% | 10% | $2,000 |
| $3.0 Million | 17.5% | 15% | $3,000 |
| $3.0 Million | 20% | 21.75% | $4,350 |
| $3.5 Million | 20% | 24% | $4,800 |

** For achieving $3.0 million revenue and 20 percent net profit there is a special "kicker" bonus of 2.5 percent of salaries over and above the other bonuses, or 4 percent additional bonus for achieving $3.5 million revenue and 20 percent net profit.

We are very excited about our Goal 97 the financial benefits to you and HSM could be incredible!

We would like to make a payout semiannually. This year, our semiannual payout date is right around the corner. Because we are still learning, we are setting the amount of the semiannual payout at 10 percent of the total bonus earned, based on our 6-month numbers. Since we do not know what the next 6 months will bring, we are being very conservative. The remaining 90 percent of the bonus amount rolls over to the next six month portion of Goal 97. If we continue at our current rate, all of us could have a very profitable year!

Please review this memo and the attached worksheets. We will field questions and further explain the numbers during the staff meeting on Tuesday at 10 AM. Please bring this memo, your questions, and "what-ifs" with you. Keep the business coming, the jobs profitable and the expenses under control! We all have a lot to gain!

*LTQ must reach a minimum cash balance of $350,000, plus bonuses, profit sharing, and 401K matching at year-end, and a minimum profit of $300,000 at year-end.*

| Profit Bonuses | Revenue Amounts less than $2.0M | $2.0M | $2.5M | $3.0M | $3.5M |
|---|---|---|---|---|---|
| Profit Levels | | | | | |
| Less than 16% | 0.00% | 0.00% | 0.00% | 0.00% | 0.00% |
| 16% of Revenue | 0.00% | 2.00% | 8.50% | 8.50% | 8.50% |
| 17.5% of Revenue | 0.00% | 5.00% | 12.75% | 12.75% | 12.75% |
| 20% of Revenue | 0.00% | 9.00% | 17.00% | 19.50% | 21.00% |

| Revenue Bonuses | Profit Levels Less than 16% | 16% | 17.5% | 20% |
|---|---|---|---|---|
| Revenue Amounts | | | | |
| Less than $2.5M | 0.00% | 0.00% | 0.00% | 0.00% |
| $2.5M | 0.00% | 1.50% | 1.50% | 1.50% |
| $3.0M | 0.00% | 2.25% | 2.25% | 2.25% |
| $3.5M | 0.00% | 3.00% | 3.00% | 3.00% |

| The LTQ Group | Revenues at $3.5M—Salaries estimated at $1.15 Million | | |
|---|---|---|---|
| Bonus 3.xls | ESTIMATED Profit at 16% of Revenue | ESTIMATED Profit at 17.5% of Revenue | ESTIMATED Profit at 20% of Revenue |
| Revenue | $3,500,000 | $3,500,000 | $3,500,000 |
| PROFIT | $560,000 | $612,500 | $700,000 |
| Threshold at 7% of revenues for capital investment, return on owner's investment, discretionary | $245,000 | $245,000 | $245,000 |
| Revenue bonus 3% of salaries of $1.15M | $34,500 | $34,500 | $34,500 |
| Profit bonus 8.5%, 12.75%, 17% of salaries | $97,750 | $145,625 | $195,500 |
| Special bonus for $3.5M revenues at 20% profits, 4% of salaries | | | $46,000 |
| SUBTOTAL BONUSES | $132,250 | $181,125 | $275,000 |
| Total bonus as a % of salary | 11.50% | 15.75% | 24.00% |
| PROFIT LESS THRESHOLD LESS BONUSES | $182,750 | $186,375 | $179,000 |
| Estimated profit-sharing contribution | $80,000 | $80,000 | $80,000 |
| Estimated profit sharing as a % of salary | 6.96% | 6.96% | 6.96% |
| Estimated matching contribution | $18,000 | $18,000 | $18,000 |
| Estimated matching as a % of salary | 1.57% | 1.57% | 1.57% |
| TAXABLE PROFITS | $84,760 | $88,375 | $81,000 |
| Total estimated benefits: Bonuses, profit sharing, and matching as a % of salary | 20.02% | 24.27% | 32.52% |

| The LTQ Group | Revenues at $3.0M—Salaries estimated at $1.1 Million | | |
|---|---|---|---|
| Bonus 3.xls | ESTIMATED Profit at 16% of Revenue | ESTIMATED Profit at 17.5% of Revenue | ESTIMATED Profit at 20% of Revenue |
| Revenue | $3,000,000 | $3,000,000 | $3,000,000 |
| PROFIT | $480,000 | $525,000 | $600,000 |
| Threshold at 7% of revenues for capital investment, return on owner's investment, discretionary | $210,000 | $210,000 | $210,000 |
| Revenue bonus 2.25% of salaries —$1.1M | $24,750 | $24,750 | $24,750 |
| Profit bonus 8.5%, 12.75%, 17% of salaries | $93,500 | $140,250 | $187,000 |
| Special bonus for $3.0M revenues at 20% profits, 2.5% of salaries | | | $27,500 |
| SUBTOTAL BONUSES | $118,250 | $165,000 | $239,250 |
| Total bonus as a % of salary | 10.75% | 15.00% | 21.75% |
| PROFIT LESS THRESHOLD LESS BONUSES | $151,750 | $150,000 | $150,750 |
| Estimated profit-sharing contribution | $80,000 | $80,000 | $80,000 |
| Estimated profit sharing as a % of salary | 7.27% | 7.27% | 7.27% |
| Estimated matching contribution | $18,000 | $18,000 | $18,000 |
| Estimated matching as a % of salary | 1.84% | 1.64% | 1.64% |
| TAXABLE PROFITS | $53,750 | $52,000 | $52,750 |
| Total estimated benefits: Bonuses, profit sharing, and matching as a % of salary | 19.66% | 23.91% | 30.66% |

| The LTQ Group | Revenues at $2.5M—Salaries estimated at $1.05 Million | | |
|---|---|---|---|
| Bonus 3.xls | ESTIMATED Profit at 16% of Revenue | ESTIMATED Profit at 17.5% of Revenue | ESTIMATED Profit at 20% of Revenue |
| Revenue | $2,500,000 | $2,500,000 | $2,500,000 |
| PROFIT | $400,000 | $437,500 | $500,000 |
| Threshold at 7% of revenues for capital investment, return on owner's investment, discretionary | $175,000 | $175,000 | $175,000 |
| Revenue bonus 1.5% of salaries —$1.05M | $15,750 | $15,750 | $15,750 |
| Profit bonus 8.5%, 12.75%, 17% of salaries | $89,250 | $133,875 | $178,500 |
| SUBTOTAL BONUSES | $105,000 | $149,625 | $194,250 |
| Total bonus as a % of salary | 10.00% | 14.25% | 18.50% |
| PROFIT LESS THRESHOLD LESS BONUSES | $120,000 | $112,875 | $130,750 |
| Estimated profit-sharing contribution | $70,000 | $70,000 | $70,000 |
| Estimated profit sharing as a % of salary | 6.67% | 6.67% | 6.67% |
| Estimated matching contribution | $16,000 | $16,000 | $16,000 |
| Estimated matching as a % of salary | 1.52% | 1.52% | 1.52% |
| TAXABLE PROFITS | $34,000 | $26,875 | $44,750 |
| Total estimated benefits: Bonuses, profit sharing, and matching as a % of revenue | 18.19% | 22.44% | 26.69% |

| The LTQ Group | Revenues at $2.0M—Salaries estimated at $1.05 Million | | |
|---|---|---|---|
| Bonus 3.xls | ESTIMATED Profit at 16% of Revenue | ESTIMATED Profit at 17.5% of Revenue | ESTIMATED Profit at 20% of Revenue |
| Revenue | $2,000,000 | $2,000,000 | $2,000,000 |
| PROFIT | $320,000 | $350,000 | $400,000 |
| Threshold at 9% of revenues for capital investment, return on owner's investment, discretionary | $180,000 | $180,000 | $180,000 |
| Revenue bonus 0% of salaries —$1.05M | $0 | $0 | $0 |
| Profit bonus 2%, 5%, 9% of salaries | $21,000 | $52,500 | $94,500 |
| SUBTOTAL BONUSES | $21,000 | $52,500 | $94,500 |
| Total bonus as a % of salary | 2.00% | 5.00% | 9.00% |
| PROFIT LESS THRESHOLD LESS BONUSES | $119,000 | $117,500 | $125,500 |
| Estimated profit-sharing contribution | $70,000 | $70,000 | $70,000 |
| Estimated profit sharing as a % of salary | 6.67% | 6.67% | 6.67% |
| Estimated matching contribution | $16,000 | $16,000 | $16,000 |
| Estimated matching as a % of salary | 1.52% | 1.52% | 1.52% |
| TAXABLE PROFITS | $33,000 | $31,500 | $39,500 |
| Total estimated benefits: Bonuses, profit sharing, and matching as a % of revenue | 10.19% | 13.19% | 17.19% |

## EXAMPLE 2

### No-Kidding Ownership Bonus Systems

Schrock Cabinet Company, headquartered in Dublin, Ohio, has $200 million in sales and 1500 employees at its six locations.

To align employee pay with company vision and values, management enacted the following incentive pay system. Like many open-book companies, financial education parallels the introduction of the pay-for-performance success-sharing plan.

### *Schrock Cabinet Company Success-Sharing Plan*

**Purpose:** To provide all regular, full-time SCC associates (salaries and hourly) a stake in the outcome of the business so that all associates become actively engaged in the processes that contribute to business success. It is the goal of this success-sharing plan to:

- Share the rewards of the business with those who create it,
- Provide focus on the key measurements critical to the organization's business,
- Create active involvement by tapping into the capabilities of all associates,
- Create change needed for continuous improvement in work processes and communications systems while keeping an intense focus on business goals,
- Create big picture, systems thinking,
- Help all associates think like owners,
- Provide an environment consistent with the SCC and Electrolux Vision and Values, and
- Provide an environment with people having fun and enjoying the challenges.

It is not the purpose of this plan to debate, recommend, or change the methodology of how expenses/charges are transferred and/or allocated between or among sites. The focus is to encourage behavior that identifies true improvement or cost reduction.

**Scope:** All full-time, regular associates of Schrock Cabinet Company.

**Effective Dates:** This plan will be based on the period from July 1, 1996, through December 31, 1996, for site goals, and January 1, 1996, through December 31, 1996, for profitability goals.

**Funding:** This plan will be self-funded, that is, all pay-outs under the plan will be funded by improved financial results as indicated.

**Success-Sharing Pool:** OPII (Operating Profits before taxes and interest) will be shared with associates when a pool of funds is created based upon the location's results (see location's plan and examples). Locational results will be used in 1996 to push accountability to the locations for business success, and create ownership of the location's results. The pool will have two components: OPII profitability is 50 percent of potential payout, and the achievement of specific site goals is the other 50 percent. Profitability component will be paid to all associates of that location if OPII goals are achieved. The site goals component will be paid if the associate's site achieved target in quality, delivery, and safety and OPII goals are met. Each of the site goals components is worth one-third of the total site goals payout potential ($\frac{1}{3}$ of 50%).

Pool amounts will be divided by total payroll and expressed as a percentage of W-2 base pay, shift premium, and overtime earnings each associate receives. Any payout generated under the plan will be paid in the first quarter of 1997.

**Site Goals:**

- These will be measures that indicate how well the site satisfies its customer(s), whether internal or external, in the areas of quality, delivery, and safety.
- Each of the three goals should reflect continuous improvement from a baseline measure. If the target is met, that part of the success-sharing pool will be paid if OPII goals are met.

The goals for the period of July 1, 1996, through December 31, 1996, are as follows:

- **Quality:** Achieve Inventory Record Accuracy (IRA) of 96 percent from 7/1/96–12/31/96.
- **Delivery:** Achieve order completion rate of 98 percent from 7/1/96–12/31/96.

- **Safety:** Achieve 5 percent improvement in Lost-Time Incident Case Rate from 7/1/96–12/31/96 over a base period of full year 1995 results.

**Payouts:** If the plan generates a success-sharing pool, Payouts will be during the first quarter of 1997. Any amounts already paid during 1996 under a gainsharing/production bonus plan will be deducted from the total payout. The amount for each associate will be determined by the following:

- Pool dollars divided by total payroll (hourly and salary, including overtime and shift premium) times associate's W-2 earnings. Example: Pool dollars generated are $250,000. Total payroll for the period is $8,000,000. 250,000/8,000,000 = 3.125 percent. An associate in this example who earned $20,000 during 1996 would receive 3.125 percent of $20,000 which is $625.00, payable in the first quarter of 1997 as his or her success sharing payout (minus any amount paid in 1996 under production bonus or gain-sharing plan).

**Eligibility:**

- SCC Associates must be on the payroll as an active associate December 31, 1996, to be eligible for payout, except for associates who retire or die, in which case the associate (or the associate's estate or heirs in case of death) will receive a prorated payout.
- Associates who retire or died prior to the effective date of this plan (July 1, 1996) are not eligible to participate.
- New hires will participate beginning with their first day of work.
- Those not on active employment status on December 31, 1996, or later must be actively returned to work prior to date of payout to receive payout.
- Associates who are responsible for results at more than one location will participate with portions of their salaries allocated to the locations supported. Payout percentage will be applied to the portion of their salary allocated to each location supported.

**Review/Update:** This SCC Success-Sharing Plan will be reviewed at least annually and may be revoked or revised at any time.

# Appendix II

## About the Survey

Capital Connections designed a data-gathering survey for the purpose of getting specific answers to a variety of questions about how companies introduce and experience open-book management:

- Why they do it.
- What results they have seen.
- What difficulties they have had in implementation.
- What specific techniques and methods they have used for training.

Surveys, well-designed and considered, can generate great data. They can shed light on situations that are filled with information gaps, secrets, and speculation. And surveys can also raise another set of questions. This survey did both.

## Who Took the Survey

Managers, 101 of them, mostly CEOs and a few in other senior management positions, of 97 different-sized companies in the United States and Canada filled out the survey. These companies combined are responsible for more than $6.3 billion in sales and employ more than 31,000 employees.

We thought it important to include some companies who had only a marginal knowledge, if any, of open-book management. Seeing how certain practices, like variable pay, could be spreading into open-book and non-open-book companies would be of value. Of the 97 companies surveyed, 15 CEOs said they had no working knowledge of open-book, although some of these were attempting to communicate financial information to their employees anyway.

The Executive Committee (TEC), a 40-year-old San Diego company whose mission is the enhancement of the lives and businesses of 3,500 CEOs in the United States, agreed to send out the survey to several hundred members for their response. Some 70-plus TEC companies responded, and most of those are in the growth sector of the small and mid-sized companies with fewer than 500 employees (and of this survey's respondents, 70% were less than 100).

The industries represented were totally, if not equally mixed, reflecting the larger number of service companies as a whole in the economy:

- In manufacturing.
- In distribution.
- In various service environments.

Most are not technology companies, and they spread very evenly geographically from the rust belt to the sun belt. Most are also from larger cities, since most TEC CEOs are in business in big cities.

Many TEC members are *INC.* readers and so the survey is probably biased in the direction of those small businesses that already know about business literacy, having found open-book management a fairly common *INC.* subject for years. And TEC itself has promoted open-book management concepts to its membership through seminars and mailings.

In addition to TEC companies, our firm, Capital Connections sent out surveys to our 15 biggest clients, most of them public companies with sales of more than $500 million. The input received from these large companies, 17 in all since we sent to more than one person per company, make up the remainder of the responses. Like most other features of big companies, different divisions and facilities vary enormously in their use and understanding of open-book management. Not all respondents answered 100 percent of the questions, and so on any particular item there may have been 85 responses instead of 101.

The survey categorized company size by number of employees:

- Less than 100/72 of these.
- Over 100/29 of these.

rather than by sales, since the size of the workforce and the training and communication systems that have to be in place vary more by number of employees than by sales volume. And since most respondents were in the less than 100 employee category, most were also privately and not publicly held.

We combined the data on the large companies with privately held companies of over 100 total employees for a simple reason—*the large companies are generally implementing open-book management one facility at a time.* A large utility like Central and Southwest will have more resources than a small Acme Products and will go to the corporate till for its capital expenditures, not its banker. But an open-book Central and Southwest power generation plant will, for educational and information-sharing purposes, look more like a small open-book Acme Products than a more traditional Central and Southwest plant.

Coupled with this survey, our extensive client work inside of 40 large corporations, including hundreds of hours of data-gathering interviews, seminars, facilitated meetings, and coaching, we can make observations about open-book management inside big companies that stem from more than the survey alone.

Many of the respondents were open to further discussions about open-book management with us and we followed up the survey with phone calls to gain more insight into the particulars of their experience with open-book management.

## OVERALL SURVEY RESULTS

The new technologies of open-book have been infiltrating the workplace at varying levels of intensity across most every industry (perhaps healthcare, is the one exception) with a wide range of mostly positive results.

The survey data supported what was already known by some observers, that:

- Top managers embrace the concept before it can fly.
- Financial education is the single most important facet to get started, and it is difficult to design well.
- Bonuses are being used to get employees to think like business people, but the education and communication systems to support the bonus are lagging.

- The results of open-book practices yield a variety of positive outcomes, tangible and operational, and those more tied to the human spirit of work, like pride.
- Most companies are still relatively new at doing this.
- Books and training and bonuses are the key aids to creating the new collective mentality and culture of business literate companies.

The data support the notion that in small companies, those under 100 employees, immediate teamwork improvements are the common outcome of open-book practices. In the larger companies, accountability and pride were just as highly ranked as teamwork.

The causal chain of events goes something like this:

- Open-books and line-of-sight create accountability by making visible formerly hidden and misunderstood feedback loops.
- The accountability for results creates a challenge most employees respond to positively, and their sense of pride increases as they make the business happen.
- The increase in pride raises the collective commitment and thinking of the teams and now the big picture outlook of teamwork and customer value and entrepreneurial thinking takes over.
- Once business thinking begins, the rewards of the variable pay system kick in, providing a regular reminder that the process never ends and that you are only as good as the last quarter—continuous improvement becomes a given.

Now let's look at the details of the survey that support our findings and interpretations. For the broad-brush readers, the following has far too much nit-picky stuff, and for the data-hounds of the world, not enough.

For us, the survey was taxing in its detail, fun in its interpretation, and a good start for understanding the dynamics of open-book practices and implementation.*

## *What the Survey Covered*

The survey covered the key areas of open-book practice and requested advice and information that most companies want to know about as they embark upon or deepen their journey into business literacy. These included:

- Company demographics.
- Ownership structure.
- Familiarity with open-book management.

The exact questions related to:

- Type of business.
- Annual sales revenues.
- Number of employees.
- Ownership: public or private.
- Familiarity in the form of . . .

---

*The norm group for this survey is too small to be considered strictly scientific. However, statistician Don Goldenbaum, PhD and CEO of Applied Communications Group Inc., a technical communication company in Overland Park, Kansas, states that the survey is valuable and informative for several reasons:

- "The results of the survey cut new ground. It provides a first glimpse of just how much today's managers know about and practice open-book management, and provides insights on differences among companies of different sizes and different lengths of practice.
- The data "jell." The findings seem well-defined and internally consistent and are in line with the common wisdom in the field that is beginning to take hold.
- The survey points in the direction of what should be investigated next, identifying potential areas of need among companies wanting to do open-book management."

The following describes my familiarity with open-book management (also known as business literacy).

| | Less Than 100 Employees | 100 Plus | Total |
|---|---|---|---|
| Extremely familiar | 17 | 10 | 27 |
| Vaguely familiar | 33 | 10 | 43 |
| Moderately familiar | 10 | 2 | 12 |
| Never head of open-book management | 10 | 5 | 15 |

## *Comparing Companies Skills in the Different Systems—What Do Open-Book Companies Try First?*

Perhaps the question that was the single most informing of the survey was number 7. The survey asked respondents to record, on a scale of 1 to 10, how far into the practices of open-book management they were.* It was the following:

#7. Plot your company's current practices of open-book management on these scales:

**Using and understanding Critical Numbers**

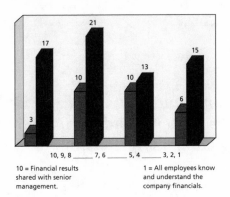

10, 9, 8 _____ 7, 6 _____ 5, 4 _____ 3, 2, 1

10 = Financial results shared with senior management.

1 = All employees know and understand the company financials.

---

*The data captured by question 7 was presented in the book chapters in smaller chunks—No-Kidding Ownership in the chapter on bonuses and motivation (Chapter 7), for example.

The best way to see all the data gathered by this question is to see the three different practices in immediate comparison to each other. That is how it is presented here.

**Intensive Huddle Systems practices of forecasting numbers and results against a plan**

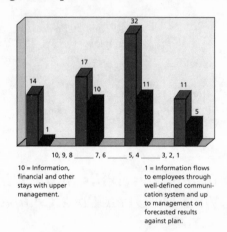

10 = Information, financial and other stays with upper management.

1 = Information flows to employees through well-defined communication system and up to management on forecasted results against plan.

**No-Kidding Ownership practices of variable pay**

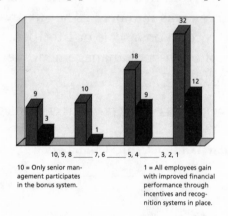

10 = Only senior management participates in the bonus system.

1 = All employees gain with improved financial performance through incentives and recognition systems in place.

## *The Most Common Beginning Practice Is to Put in Bonus Systems and Variable Pay in No-Kidding Ownership Fashion.*

Well over half of the respondents scored their company as having in place a bonus and variable pay system, that when company financial goals are accomplished, impacts the paychecks of most of their employees. More than a third said all employees are included in the plan.

Only 10 percent said that incentives were for executives only.

**This represents a sea change over the last 10 years in compensation practices.** In the early 1980s, most employees across America (surveyed by Yankelovich and others) believed that when they worked harder and better someone else would get the pay-off. Things are not that way anymore, for the companies in this survey, and we suspect for most others, as incentive pay has been on the rise.

Our contention is, however, that the bonus system, as hard as it is to do well (it does get better with practice) is just the beginning of open-book management. When tied to line-of-sight financial know-how, and accountable forecasting against a plan by teams, then the real pay-off for the bonus will hit.

## *Huddles and Critical Number Know-How Take Longer to Implement than Bonuses*

Even the companies that scored themselves highly on reward systems (Figure 3–2), scored themselves only slightly better than average on people knowing and understanding the numbers and on teams forecasting their own numbers to management for variances against the plan.

As an example, in the company-size category of less than 100 employees, 32 of 69 responding companies scored themselves near the top in bonuses and incentives. But only 15 scored themselves near the top in employees knowing the numbers and 11 in forecasting the numbers against the plan.

This tells us that while the reward structure may be in place to support the learning, that the next open-book field to plow is in the education and communication arena, so employees can take full advantage of the bonus system in place.

## *CEOs Initiate Open-Book Management*

Of all the survey questions, this came out the clearest: The overwhelming majority of initiators of open-book management for a company is the CEO.

Who in the organization was responsible for initiating the practices of OBM?

CEO    55

Senior Level Management—

| HR  3 | Operations  6 | Quality  2 | Training  3 |
|-------|---------------|------------|-------------|

This is not a surprise. In many ways, the CEO is the only position that can truly sponsor open-book management in its fullest form because of all the required coordination between departments. And remember the survey was sent to and answered by CEOs.

There were certain exceptions. The operations managers came in a distant second to the CEOs. Then 3 training directors, 2 quality directors, 3 organization effectiveness managers, and 3 HR managers were the instigators at their companies.

Where were the financial managers?

We don't know.

But we do have a couple of explanations.

First, many small companies don't have a financial officer.

But what about the bigger companies? We have worked with many financial managers in the Critical Numbers Know-how arena. It is financial literacy—getting employees to understand the company financial reports, the costing, the billing, business development and the budget systems that make up the numbers. CFOs are the number one sponsor of this kind of financial learning, which then acts as one of the underpinnings to full-blown open-book management. But these CFOs see themselves more as sponsoring a kind of training than implementing open-book management.

## Motivation: Why Do Companies Choose to Move Toward Business Literacy?

Two overwhelming reasons for using open-book management* clearly emerged from the survey:

- Strengthens teamwork across the company.
- A belief in the philosophy by upper management.

These responses have clear implications, and also raise some more interesting questions.

We gave nine options to survey respondents on why they chose to pursue open-book practices, five on the pain-avoiding side of the motivation equation and four on the goal-seeking side:

We are motivated to incorporate OBM due to: (Check all applicable)

|  | *Under 100* | *Over 100* | *TOTAL* |
|---|---|---|---|
| Profitability problems | 13 | 2 | 15 |
| Communication/trust problems | 12 | 7 | 19 |
| Current programs failing | 4 | 1 | 5 |
| Productivity problems | 9 | 1 | 10 |
| Cash flow problems | 6 | 2 | 8 |
| To improve customer service | 20 | 13 | 33 |
| To maintain competitive advantage | 19 | 18 | 37 |
| To strengthen teamwork | 35 | 18 | 53 |
| Belief in the philosophy | 36 | 20 | 56 |

Over half the respondents chose teamwork and philosophy as motivations. And there were some noteworthy runner-ups.

**It is our contention, based on the observations afforded us by our work, that an ounce of open-book management can do more to create teamwork, than a**

---

*Part of this company motivation data was presented in Chapter Three—Why Do You Want To Do This?

**pound of team-building and even team-structuring can.** One reason for this—the big picture that a team needs to pull together.

It is another contention that if leaders are not attracted to the philosophy—the underlying belief system—of open-book management, then it won't work. One question we will keep asking: What part of the philosophy is the most compelling to you? For one company it might be the accountability, for another, the sense of generating and sharing the wealth, for another, the joy of learning.

That's for the next survey. In the meantime, it is clear that leaders who see the rich set of underlying beliefs in open-book systems will adopt the practices because they resonate with their own beliefs.

The next two most frequently mentioned reasons for adopting business literacy practices were:

- To maintain competitive advantage.
- To improve customer service.

These motivations are clearly on the strategic versus the tactical level, *pointing to the practical/doable facets of open-book management as an underpinning for getting the business where it needs to be.* Making all employees business thinkers is clearly a superior way to educate and motivate the company to perform competitively for the long term. The financial emphasis in open-book management highlights the record of how customers decide they want to do business, and how efficiently the company goes about that task.

The motivations mentioned the least are the five pain-avoiding ones, which may say something about motivation in general. Companies with cash flow and profit problems were less than 10 percent of the respondents. Communication and trust problems were mentioned about the same frequency and fewer still were those whose primary motivations were productivity and programs that were currently not working.

The rather low showing for profitability and cash flow motives fits with the notion that business literacy is really about making good companies better, that maintaining competitive advantage is more common than trying to get one. But there were notable exceptions—open-book practices have been used in turn-around situations.

## *The Financial, Operational, and Intangible Benefits That the Companies Report*

The survey listed 10 benefits to choose from (and respondents were encouraged to check up to four). The financial benefits had a follow-up question covered in the next item. There was also a "too early to say" response for the companies at it for less than a year, which only 9 companies checked.

Responses across all categories recorded 249 benefits for the 80 practicing companies and went like this—keep in mind the motivation for companies to do this as you read.

|  | *Under 100* | *Over 100* | TOTAL |
|---|---|---|---|
| Improved financial results | 11 | 11 | 22 |
| Better at managing change | 14 | 8 | 22 |
| More entrepreneurial thinking | 13 | 13 | 26 |
| Clearer responsibility and accountability | 22 | 12 | 34 |
| Improved employee pride and morale | 22 | 5 | 27 |
| More reliable, systematic communication | 8 | 4 | 12 |
| More effective alignment of company results with compensation programs | 18 | 13 | 31 |
| Better financial forecasting | 5 | 6 | 11 |
| Better business thinking | 12 | 13 | 25 |
| Stronger teamwork | 23 | 15 | 38 |

The clear winners, above 30—teamwork, pride, and alignment of results to compensation programs—all fall in the operational and intangible benefits category.

The front-runner teamwork, stems from the big-picture open-books provide. In second place and supporting teamwork is clearer accountability and responsibility, one of the underpinnings of the open-book approach. When the financials are open for regular reporting of results, the sales and the cost and expense numbers come home to roost on departments and the teams and even the individuals who are most accountable for making the numbers happen. Hiding numbers hides results, mistakes, trends, customer reaction, and just about everything else. Sharing numbers, when practiced consistently and with education, creates the culture of accountability necessary for high performance.

The other top two—pride and alignment of results with compensation—are major, predictable, universal results of what open-book cultures create.

The survey confirms what the early adopters have been willing to try without much evidence. With the accountability and feedback of rich open-book information systems and their connection to the marketplace and to the other departments in the company, increases in pride automatically accompany employees' seeing the impact of their efforts. Teamwork increases because the financial results demand across-department whole-company, coordinated effort.

For the 22 companies practicing open-book management for longer than three years, the teamwork benefit was listed by 16. And their financial results also improved more regularly than companies those practicing for shorter lengths of time.

## *Financial Impact of Open-Books: It's Still Early and the News Is Good*

A 46% average growth rate for 14 years.

The unit cost per barrel of oil dropping from $17.17 to $13.64

Profitability going from:

| | | |
|---|---|---|
| 1% | to | 5% |
| 5% | to | 12% |
| 8% | to | 11% |
| 3% | to | 6% |
| 11% | to | 16% |

increasing 30% the first year

Debt to Equity going from  1.02/1  to  .37/1
2.5/1   to  1.8/1

These are some of the financial results reported from the survey. The exact survey item was:

Specifically, we've seen the following key financial numbers or ratios change largely as a result of open-book management approaches:

Profitability          From: _____ to: _____
Debt to Equity:          _____
Other (specify):          _____
No measureable changes seen to date: _____

No company reported a downturn in their financial performance. But a large number of companies, some 60 percent (see last section on benefits) did not report financial improvements as part of their benefits, nor did they supply information on financial results of any kind. By not answering this question it might be possible to assume that:

- They were looking for other results first, like teamwork.
- They were not willing to attribute solely to open-book management the good or the bad financial news.

- Financial results are often not a lead indicator of how well open-book management is going, but a lag indicator. It's what comes last, not first.

Our experience and common sense tells us that the small companies are the ones that experience the most immediate financial results from open-book practices, making comments like the above "30 percent increase in profits the first year" possible.

Most leaders avoid the folly of attributing any one thing all the credit for a positive change. The broker who wants to take credit for a 30 percent increase in the value of your portfolio after a year like 1995, when 30 percent was the norm, won't have much credibility. Life and business events, we all learn, are multicausal.

Market turns, competitor moves, and a whole host of issues can do more to increase or decrease financial results than open-book management. But the long-term open-book companies are, like good investors, thinking of results over time. And a motivated company of business thinkers can take some of the steepness out of the marketplace valleys and ramp up the good times to maximize and stabilize the business.

The survey gathered more data on profit than other financial measures. Profitability is the most common financial measure to attack for start up open-book companies. For most industries, healthy balance sheets usually are the offshoot of years of good profit, and employees can learn the most by first seeing their impact on profits and then learning the balance sheet measures.

Should a company expect early financial gains as a result of open-book practices? It depends on several things, size perhaps the biggest of the factors, along with a host of others.

If a quality process, for instance, had a good cost of quality measure and employees have already been asked to watch process costs, most of the low hanging financial fruit may have already been picked. If, however, business literacy efforts are the first legitimate involvement effort, the company can expect to harvest the financial gains of cost containment much earlier.

## Financial Training and Books Aid in the Implementation

The survey listed several tools and aids a company could use to get their open-book management processes started. We included:

|                             | Less than 100 | 100–500 | TOTAL |
|-----------------------------|---------------|---------|-------|
| Financial training          | 24            | 11      | 35    |
| Obm seminars/workshops      | 9             | 10      | 19    |
| Obm planning                | 8             | 8       | 16    |
| Books                       | 26            | 14      | 40    |
| Field visits                | 2             | 6       | 8     |
| Software                    | 8             | 10      | 18    |
| Incentive and bonus systems | 29            | 18      | 47    |

The most used aids were books, financial training, and bonus systems. The bonus system was not a surprise given the earlier findings.

Books were also very near the top of the aids used. The reaction we continue to get on the practical nature of our first book, *The Power of Open-Book Management*, with its emphasis on planning and implementation, convinces us that even in a high-tech world books are as good, if not better than, most media for people to mull over the necessary thoughts to go a new direction.

Field visits to open-book companies were down on the list, as was software. Open-book seminars were used minimally, and open-book planning, a high-involvement process for teaching employees the business by bringing them into the plan, which just happens to make a better plan in the process, was also not used very much (only 14 companies said they use planning as an aid).

This again tells us that companies are early into the process and the more sophisticated systems/aids like planning are going to come. Again, what we find is that companies consider sharing financial information the essence of open-book management. While this is the necessary step to get started, the real organizational capability business literacy affords is much more about teams of employees managing and creating their future by constantly looking ahead and meeting or exceeding plans of their own making.

The survey asked a few fill-in-the-blank questions. One of them was: "What have been the easiest and most difficult parts of implementing open-book management?"

The responses to this part of the survey fall into several major catagories. The *difficult* parts most frequently included:

- Educating all employees on the financials.
- Implementing the right measures and having the right cost control data: without it the accountability won't happen.
- Time constraints for planning the education and communication strategy and doing the training.
- Communicating the results across geography, shifts and other barriers.

## Many of the comments were telling.

"Convincing my management team," showing that CEOs can't manage open-book systems by edict.

"Maintaining the enthusiasm," indicating humans can get bored with anything after a while.

"People didn't believe they could achieve the needed targets," resisting accountability for someone else's targets is very common. and . . .

"It takes a lot of the CEO's time"

"Getting managers to share negative information."

And one of our favorites, perhaps because it is too true.

"If a lot of trust already exists, people would prefer not to know when things are not good."

The number of *easy* things about implementing open-book management equaled the number of difficult, so that was encouraging. And what some listed as most difficult, others listed as easy:

- Getting the numbers out to everybody.
- Describing the bonus.
- Getting managers to share positive information.
- People buying into the concept right away.
- Passing out bonuses.

The easy parts usually included either some part of the early stages when concepts and communicating were the products. Or any time there was good news, the ease and fun of celebrating and sharing came through.

Of note, only two companies listed designing the bonus system was easy and no company said financial education was easy.

## AND IF YOU ARE NOT USING OPEN-BOOK MANAGEMENT PRACTICES

Finally, the survey asked those respondents that weren't using open-book management to supply a reason as to why.

Of the 15 who said they weren't at all into open-book practices, 12 said they didn't know what it was.

Our interpretation of this, which we did not spend a lot of time on, was that it was very hard, indeed impossible, to say that you are using something when you don't know what that something is. And for that answer, we thanked our honest, but obviously befuddled respondents, who received a three-page, multi-item survey by fax, with the request to respond quickly, on something that they did not know existed.

Oh, well!!

# *Appendix III*

## AN ECONOMIST'S VIEW OF OPEN-BOOK MANAGEMENT

Open-book management is a tool that is particularly relevant to the increasing pace of global economic change and the emergence of new economies transitioning from various forms of central planning and control. The most consistent difference between the style of capitalism in the United States and that which is practiced in much of the rest of the world is the interaction between the economic players and social/government needs. While companies in the United States have tended to focus exclusively on their stockholders and owners and have defined their mission according to what best meets the needs of this group, many companies in Europe, Asia, and Latin America have been expected to play a much greater social role. Governments, unions, social organizations, and the overall culture of many nations demand that the business community become integrated in the goals of the entire system they are part of. The use of open-book management is ideally suited for systems in which accurate information needs to be shared with a larger community. By involving the employees, the interested community, and the other stakeholders, the business is able to communicate their goals and their accomplishments.

In the case of the transition economies of what were once East Europe and the USSR, the use of open-book management is essential. These cultures are still grappling with what capitalism actually means while trying to throw off decades of distrust toward business. As they emerge from socialism, they have been victimized by unscrupulous people who have twisted the free market to serve their selfish interests. In many cases, the old "apparatchiks" who grew up in the bureaucratically stifling environment of the old Soviet Union became the "new" capitalists but they ran the system in the same way they had in the past. The organization was hierarchic and based on exploitation, leading the population to become disillusioned, blaming capitalism itself for the blunders and rapaciousness of the new business owners. The challenge faced by business in this new environment is to reestablish faith in a system based on free market principles while converting the workers from resentful, unproductive drones into productive, motivated employees. By communicating clearly what the company is doing and why, management can begin to dispel the distrust. What the workers in these systems have lacked for decades is any form of objective understanding. Through the process of open-book management they can finally see what their role in the process actually is and why it matters if they do a good job or not. For perhaps the first time in their working lives they may be able to link what they are with a larger whole, whether that is the company, the community, or the entire nation they are a part of.

In the developed nations of Western Europe, a different issue is the focus. These countries and the industries within them are tied to common aspirations and community goals. In France, Germany, Italy, Great Britain, Spain, and many others, the culture holds that business is not apart from the community. Unions have much greater political and economic influence, government plays a much more directive role and social norms are such that companies must always consider the impact of their decisions on the rest of the environment they inhabit. Given these demands, it is imperative that business be able to communicate clearly what is happening within it and what its intentions might be. The use of open-book management allows unions to feel fully informed and gives the community an insight into what is taking place and why. It removes much of the suspicion and misunderstanding which can paralyze business decision making.

The Asian economies are surging in the 1990s and are doing so from a tradition of consensus-based decision making in which all decisions are subjected to a careful group process. Open-book management spreads this technique even wider through allowing the active and knowledgeable participation of the entire corporate community. In past years, the hierarchy of business in these nations meant that only the senior management or senior bureaucrats in government were entitled to be involved in building this consensus, but this is changing rapidly. The rejection of dictatorial decision making has meant the emergence of democracy in Taiwan and South Korea and it has eroded the power of the Communist Party elite in Beijing as well. Japan is grafting American-style management on to their system and the result has been a flourishing of creativity and innovation.

The open-book management style has always existed in the upper echelons of Asian management and is now preparing to sweep into the rest of the organizations. As the economies of Japan, Korea, China, Malaysia, Indonesia, and others continue to grow, their styles of business will become more common in the United States and elsewhere and the use of open-book management styles will accompany this growth.

In the developing economies of Latin America, South Asia, and Africa, the concept is again connected both culturally and economically. Many of these nations experimented with various forms of socialist planning and central planning and are now in the process of abandoning them. The populations of these nations have grown disillusioned with the management styles of the past, which seemed to relegate them to a third-world status permanently. The rise of economic nationalism is demanding more communication and a more complete appreciation of what their economic options really are. The open-book management process is allowing people to rebuild trust in the free market process while motivating the employees through educating them to the realities and possibilities that exist for their industry and their community as a whole. At the same time, these nations are finding themselves at a distinct competitive disadvantage due to the long decades of inept leadership and periods of exploitation. Their search for a place in the world means that a high premium will be placed on involving the formerly disenfranchised.

The international economic system is in a constant state of flux as the next century nears. While "going global" has been the catch phrase for some time, it was never that close to a reality in the United States. We always had our own massive market to insulate us from the vagaries of the world around us. That scenario has been changing, industry by industry, as the truly global economy comes to exist. What are the implications of this "globalization" and what does open-book management have to do with the changes that can be anticipated?

To begin with, the old division of companies into categories such as multinational, transnational, international, and so on is next to useless. Nearly every company feels the impact of the global economy, directly or indirectly. Perhaps you sell your product or service to clients in other countries or perhaps you face competition from companies in other nations. Perhaps your partners now come from several different countries and are subject to delays and crises from all parts of the globe. Perhaps you are borrowing from an international bank or maybe you only sell and buy domestically, but your customers' fortunes rise and fall with the international scene. Regardless of the size or scope of your business, the global economy is a reality and this reality requires more sophisticated and consistent analysis.

The premise behind open-book management is that you have empowered your employees with knowledge and armed with the real story of their business they are able to perform better thus giving you a productivity edge. The coming decades will bring *more*, not less, competition and *more*, not less, challenge. Organizations that attempt to meet these competitors and challengers with one hand tied behind their back as a result of keeping their employees from becoming total team members, face the prospect of failure.

Beyond the obvious aspects of globalization, there is the more subtle changes taking place in the United States as our population changes. Increasingly, we are a global society within our borders with increasing percentages of citizens from Asia, Latin America, Europe, Africa, the Middle East, and elsewhere. The challenge of diversity is one that many companies are just beginning to face and fewer still are seeing diversity as the opportunity it really is. A diverse and

motivated workforce that is connected and knowledgeable about the company they are involved in will
provide that management team with the kind of
global edge that could separate dramatic success from
slow atrophy. The use of open-book management to
unite and empower that diverse work force of the future is perhaps its greatest promise.

Chris Kuehl, PhD
Economist,
The Global Group

# *Appendix IV*

## RATIONALE FOR ANSWERS TO QUIZ

1. **True.** A bankrupt company can be a profitable one.

   A company's Income Statement, using the accrual method, can show that a company has earned a profit after cost and expenses are subtracted from revenues. While at the same time, that company may not have collected revenues owed to them or for other reasons may be out of cash and therefore, unable to pay its bills.

2. **False.** In business, profit is the same as cash.

   Profit for a period of operation is calculated by subtracting revenues from expenses to arrive at net profit or net. Expenses included in this calculation can also include depreciation and amortization, which are not cash items. The net profit on an Income Statement does not indicate that the amount showing has been turned into cash.

3. **False.** Under generally accepted accounting principles, Accounts Receivable are not counted as an asset until actually collected.

   A line item under assets on the balance sheet is Accounts Receivable. This amount represents revenues that have been earned and not collected. Another line item is Cash. When an Accounts Receivable is collected, the amount collected is subtracted from the Accounts Receivables total and is added to Cash.

4. **False.** A company can operate without cash.

   Companies incur obligations to pay salaries, utilities, suppliers, etc. Cash is needed to meet these obligations. Therefore, to stay in business a company must have cash to operate. Even when companies borrow from lenders and use lines of credit to keep the business operating, this still equates to cash.

5. **True.** An Income Statement shows whether or not a company is operating profitably.

   Accountants use the approach of measuring income by measuring completed transactions during a period, thus reflecting the results of its operations during the period. The elements of an Income Statement are comprised of: Revenues, Expenses, Gains and Losses; when combined they measure the Net Income (loss). This measurement is also referred to as Profit (loss) and broadly refers to successful or unsuccessful operation during the period in which the statement covers.

6. The solvency of a company is related to **its ratio of debt to equity.**

   This is the ratio as defined by generally accepted accounting principles.

7. A company's net worth is equal to **its total assets minus its total liabilities.**

   This is the calculation defined in generally accepted accounting principles.

8. A company's equity is another name for its **Net Worth.**

   The Net Worth of a company is found on the Balance Sheet and is arrived at by subtracting all the company's debts (liabilities) from what the company owns (assets). The terms *worth* and *equity* are used interchangeably.

9. A company's profitability percentage is determined by dividing **Net Income by total Sales Revenue.**

   This calculation shows the portion of the revenue in percentage terms that the company earned after paying its expenses for that period.

10. COGS is an acronym for **Costs of Goods Sold.**

    This is standard cost accounting terminology.

# Index